Indonesia:
Church & Society

by Frank L. Cooley

FRIENDSHIP PRESS   NEW YORK

Library of Congress Catalog Card Number: 68-54899

Preface

To some people, Indonesia is fascinating. To others, it is frustrating. To those who know Indonesia best, she is both—fascinating because of the immense variety of peoples and cultures and their seemingly limitless potentialities, and frustrating because so many complex and explosive forces seem to block the attainment of national unity and stability, condemning the nation's potential to remain largely hidden.

To most Americans, however, Indonesia is known only vaguely, if at all. American Christians are always astonished to learn that the church in Indonesia is one of the oldest and largest in Asia and is very likely the most rapidly growing and vigorous church in the world today.

This book is offered as a contribution to increasing the understanding of American Christians about Indonesia in general and the church in particular. It seeks to present the life and work of the churches amid Indonesia's revolutionary development.

I have written out of the background of ten years of study and experience in this fascinating and frustrating land. Writing this book has not detracted one iota from my fascination with Indonesia; on the contrary, it has made the frustrations more understandable and acceptable, because I have seen more clearly that they are mostly rooted in the painful slowness with which potentialities can be transformed into life-enriching realities.

Most of the facts and interpretations here have been given freely to me by others. I am therefore glad to acknowledge indebtedness to the following colleagues for their criticisms and suggestions: the Reverends Pouw Ie-gan, Winburn T. Thomas, Addison J. Eastman, Myles E. Walburn; Miss Alma Guinness; and missionary colleagues in the Board of Foreign Missions of the Netherlands Reformed Church, the Rhenish Missionary Society (especially Professor Theodor Müller-Krüger), and the Basel Missionary Society.

Finally, I would like to acknowledge the encouragement and financial support of the Indonesia Committee, Asia Department, Division of Overseas Ministries of the National Council of Churches of Christ in the U.S.A.; of the Commission on Ecumenical Mission and Relations of the United Presbyterian Church in the U.S.A.; and of the Friendship Press, without whose support the book would have remained a still-born idea.

FRANK L. COOLEY

CONTENTS

BASIC FACTS ABOUT THE CHURCHES

	Name of Church	Region
1.	Indonesia Protestant Church	Indonesia
2.	*Moluccan Protestant Church* [2]	E Indo.
3.	*Timor Evangelical Christian Church*	SE Indo.
4.	*Minahasa Evangelical Christian Church*	N Sulawesi
5.	*Western Indonesia Protestant Church*	W Indo.
6.	Halmahera Evangelical Christian Church	E Indo.
7.	Sangir-Talaud Evangelical Christian Church	E Indo.
8.	*West Irian Evangelical Christian Church*	E Indo.
9.	Sumba Christian Church	SE Indo.
10.	Bali Protestant Christian Church	SE Indo.
11.	*Batak Protestant Christian Church*	N Sumatra
12.	Simalungun Protestant Christian Church	N Sumatra
13.	Karo Batak Protestant Church	N Sumatra
14.	Nias Protestant Christian Church	W Sumatra
15.	Indonesia Methodist Church	Sumatra
16.	*Kalimantan Evangelical Church*	Kalimantan
17.	Gospel Spreading Christian Church	E Kalimantan
18.	Bolaang Mongondow Evangelical Christian Church	N Sulawesi
19.	*Central Sulawesi Christian Church*	N Sulawesi
20.	*Makale-Rantepao Toradja Christian Church*	C Sulawesi
21.	Mamasa Toradja Christian Church	C Sulawesi
22.	Southeast Sulawesi Protestant Church	SE Sulawesi
23.	South Sulawesi Christian Church	S Sulawesi
24.	*East Java Christian Church*	E Java
25.	*Java Christian Churches*	C Java
26.	Java Evangelical Christian Church	C Java
27.	*Pasundan Christian Church*	W Java
28.	*East Java Indonesia Christian Church*	E Java
29.	*Central Java Indonesia Christian Church*	C Java
30.	West Java Indonesia Christian Church	W Java
31.	Church of Christ	W Java
32.	United Muria Christian Church of Indonesia	C Java
33.	Church of Jesus the Messiah	Java
34.	Bethel Full Gospel Church	Indonesia
35.	Surabaja Pentecostal Church	E Java

1 These dates are taken from Müller Krüger's book, "Sedjarah Geredja di Indonesia" (1959).
2 Churches in italics are members of the World Council of Churches.

IN THE INDONESIA COUNCIL OF CHURCHES

Date Founded[1]	Date Autonomy	Membership 1953	1967*	Percent Increase	Congregations	Ministers
(a federated body composed of 2, 3, 4 and 5)						
1534	1935	276,813	380,000	37	673	403
1612	1947	253,501	650,000	156	1,258	125
1568	1934	335,000	500,000	50	502	110
1620	1948	150,000*	350,000	1,333	89	57
1874	1949	32,140	50,000	56	240	20
1568	1947	135,000	200,000	50	275	108
1862	1956	100,000†	180,000	80	800	70
1881	1947	14,230†	31,934	125	371	44
1932	1948	2,700	6,900	155	32	17
1861	1930	650,000	819,172	26	1,365	232
1903	1963	22,000	85,257	288	208	33
1890	1940	13,808	65,000	370	200	19
1874	1936	161,565	220,000	36	390	35
1903	1964	5,961†	40,000	574	199	35
1866	1935	29,649	67,667	128	300	66
––	1962	n.a.	10,200	n.a.	41	4
1904	1950	23,729†	30,600	26	95	7
1893	1947	80,000	126,467	58	339	56
1913	1947	120,000*	185,000	54	297	43
1929	1948	20,000	40,000	100	135	7
1915	1957	3,359†	6,611	96	32	13
1851	1965	n.a.	3,500	n.a.	17	5
1815	1931	55,000*	85,000	55	79	70
1858	1931	24,813	76,500	208	149	130
1851	1940	5,565	27,000	385	16	33
1861	1934	8,234	15,500	82	40	25
1898	1934	3,000	15,000	400	9	10
1858	1945	3,580	16,000	347	26	36
1882	1940	6,714	19,785	195	30	29
1905	1940	2,662	4,000	46	8	5
1925	1925	2,200	5,000	118	12	6
1945	1945	10,617	12,000	13	12	12
n.a.	n.a.	n.a.	200,000	n.a.	n.a.	n.a.
n.a.	n.a.	n.a.	20,000	n.a.	n.a.	n.a.
TOTAL		2,551,840	4,544,093	53	8,239	1,865

* Author's best estimate, based on most accurate data available. These figures represent membership, and in some cases, constituency.
† Indonesia Council of Churches 1957 figure. (There are no generally accepted, reliable statistics based on a uniform standard.)

MAP OF INDONESIA SHOWING LOCATION OF CHURCHES

(Numbers refer to the churches described in Chapters 4 through 8 and listed in the chart, page 6.)

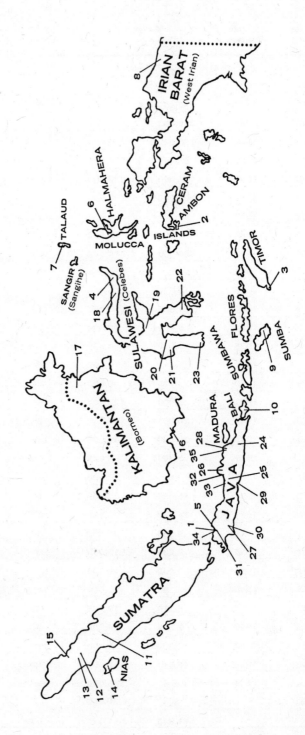

1 Indonesia Today:
The Background

A FRIEND OF MINE IS FOND OF beginning his speeches on Indonesia with the statement, "Indonesia is different." Undoubtedly, that statement is true. But to it should be added, "Indonesia is complex and unpredictable." There are good reasons why this is so, and why any person who wants to understand developments in Indonesia must be prepared to spend time and intellectual effort to determine the facts and to find an adequate framework for arranging and interpreting them. Americans generally are not familiar with the body of facts about Indonesia's history, society, culture and economic, political and religious situation. More difficult still for them is the matter of a perspective or approach that will enable the facts to be fully and rightly understood. What follows is an attempt to solve both of these difficulties.

Land and People

Indonesia is the nation born on August 17, 1945, through the proclamation of Independence from Netherlands' rule by the people of the colonial area formerly called the Dutch East Indies. What are the characteristics of this land and people today?

9

Indonesia is a farflung archipelago (see map at front of book).
Indonesians call it their *Tanah Air,* literally their "land-water." Its
territory covers 45 degrees of longitude (3,000 miles) and 17 degrees
of latitude (1,100 miles), compared with roughly 48 and 18 degrees
for the United States. Most of it, however, is water—the relatively
shallow Java and South China Seas and the much deeper Indian
Ocean, as well as the smaller Molucca, Banda and Arafura Seas. The
land area, totaling 738,865 square miles, comprises more than 3,000
islands, five of them among the world's largest.

Judged by the criteria of area, resources or population this island
nation is big. Indonesia has been well endowed by nature. Fertile
soil and abundant rainfall provide an agricultural base adequate, if
fully utilized, to produce the food, clothing and shelter needed by the
present population. The volcanic action of the mountains provides
Java and Bali with a natural and continuous process of restoring the
soil's fertility. The surrounding ocean waters are rich in fish and other
sea food, which guarantee adequate supplies of protein. The climate—
warm and wet—is ideal for relatively easy living. These conditions
provide the basis for the production of cash crops such as rubber,
coffee, tea, spices, sugar, tobacco and copra that annually earn substantial amounts of foreign exchange. In addition Indonesia possesses
significant mineral resources, abundant in the case of petroleum, tin
and bauxite, which presently constitute a major element in the
economy's export sector and offer a base for industrial development.

Indonesia's population too is big and dense. The 1961 census (the
first since 1930) surprised everyone by revealing a total of 97.8 million,
including the people of Irian Barat (formerly West New Guinea),
a figure considerably larger than was predicted by experts. The population at the end of 1966 was estimated by the government's Central
Bureau of Statistics to be 109,592,000, having increased 2.45 percent
during the year. At the time of writing, it is 112 million, making
Indonesia the fifth most populous nation in the world, next after the
United States. It is the sixth most densely peopled country in the
world. The annual rate of increase approximates 2.5 percent.

Two aspects of this population picture are particularly significant
for Indonesia's economy. First, such a rapid growth rate imposes great
pressure on the economy to expand rapidly enough not only to absorb
the annual population increase but also to accumulate sufficient capital
for continuing economic advance. In recent years the rate of annual
growth of 1.57 percent has not met this severe test.

A second critical challenge is the pronounced imbalance in population distribution, for 64.5 percent of the land's people are concentrated on the islands of Java and Madura, which comprise only 7 percent of the total land area. Population density in this central area, 1,236 people per square mile, is one of the heaviest in the world and is more than 21 times that of the rest of Indonesia. Therefore, given the present structure and level of efficiency of the economy, the provinces outside Java have insufficient population to exploit the possibilities for economic development, while Java and Madura have too many people for available opportunities. An Indonesian economist recently estimated that in 1966, 2.5 million city dwellers and between 12 and 15 million rural people were unemployed. Most of this unemployment is on Java. Such imbalance results in a situation in which the densely populated central area absorbs a much larger share of the government's expenditures than it contributes, thus creating not only economic imbalance but the possibility of political and ethnic tensions as well. Government programs in transmigration and family planning are in the right direction, but must be much larger and more effective to make headway in solving Indonesia's population problem.

Diversity and Unity

Indonesia is made up of many diverse ethnic and language groups, which have been relatively isolated from one another until quite recently. This isolation resulted from the country's marked geographic traits: deep straits and wide seas separating islands, high volcanic mountain ranges, heavy tropical rain forests and wide swampy seacoasts. These have led to differences in history, regional development, traditions, customs and religion, which accentuate the difficulty of binding these diverse groups into a unified nation. Indonesia's present condition and her main problem are symbolized by the national motto: *Bhinneka Tunggal Ika,* "Diversity Becoming Unity."

There are, on the other hand, important forces and common experiences that bind the various Indonesian peoples into one. Almost all belong to one racial stock and a single family of languages. They all live under similar geographic and climatic conditions. Most of them have experienced similar external influences over the centuries. All have lived under colonial rule, some for as long as 350 years, others for only a century. But most important of all, since 1945 they have struggled together in the revolution to attain and protect their Independence.

There is no doubt about the reality of both the unity and the diversity. The key question, as pressing for the Indonesian leaders trying to govern and develop the life of the nation as for the outsider trying to understand the country, is: Which is the growing, emerging reality—which is becoming more dominant—unity or diversity?

At times it has seemed that unity was foremost. The period of the revolutionary war against the Netherlands from 1945 to 1949 was the golden age of unity. The radical action program in early 1958 of nationalizing Dutch economic interests in response to the refusal of the Netherlands to negotiate the return of Irian Barat (New Guinea) to Indonesia was another. The period of 1959 to 1960 when the government acted to bring the retail economy, dominated by aliens, under Indonesian control was still another. Understanding the need for unity may help us comprehend the motivation for the movement back to the basic Constitution of 1945 and the "guided democracy" decreed by President Sukarno in July, 1959. At that time diversity seemed to be waxing dominant. A return to unity, or at least an attempt in that direction, was imperative. But on the crucial question of the basis of unity, there was sharp difference of opinion. It will pay us, therefore, to examine the factors that lead to diversity and make difficult the achievement of unity.

The first factor is ethnic differences. Indonesia is a highly pluralistic society. Like the United States, the nation is made up of many ethnic groups, and there is little homogeneity even within most geographic regions. On the island of Java, for instance, there are 49 million Javanese and 20 million Sundanese, who together constitute two-thirds of the population of the nation. There are in addition 15 other major ethnic groups with a membership of at least one million, each proud of its own language and culture.

Language also contributes to cultural diversity. While Indonesian is the national language used by educated people, it is not yet universal. More than 200 languages used daily in Indonesia are classified by linguists into roughly 16 major subgroups of the Malayo-Polynesian family of languages. Everyone loves his mother tongue; no one willingly sees his native language thrown on the altar as a sacrifice to cultural unity.

In the matter of customs and mores—called *adat isti adat* in Indonesian—the 3,000 islands in the Indonesian archipelago are divided by ethnologists into 19 customary law areas, each with a distinctive and autonomous system of folkways and mores. Cultural diversity is the rule; but cultural homogeneity is held up as the ideal, and there are signs it is beginning to develop in urban centers. It is clear that "the 1966 generation," the youth who forced the downfall of Sukarno, are *Indonesians* to a much greater degree than were their parents, "the 1945 generation."

Religious diversity, too, is abundantly evident. The religious picture shows the following breakdown: Muslim 85 percent, Protestant Christian 5 percent, Roman Catholic 1.2 percent, Hindu-Bali 2 percent, Buddhist 0.9 percent, animist 1.9 percent, others 4 percent. A large number of the Muslims are referred to by their leaders as *Islam statistik*, nominal Muslims. The Protestant, Roman Catholic and Hindu-Bali minorities are vigorous and self-conscious. The animists are on the defensive and rapidly declining—though their statistical decline has been accompanied by an increase in animistic elements in their adopted faiths. Indonesian religion of any sort manifests far more than a 1.9 percent animistic component! Religious diversity is the rule and is generally accepted under the *Pantja Sila*, the Five Principles underlying the Constitution. The first of these is belief in the one God and under it Islam, Christianity, Hinduism and Buddhism are recognized by the government and accorded equality and full freedom before the law. Only the very traditional minded Muslims envisage any other situation in the foreseeable future.

Many details could be added to this picture of diversity in Indonesian society. At this point, however, we must ask: Why such diversity? What is the cause of it all?

History and Change

By the end of the pre-Christian era there had come to the Indonesian archipelago several waves of immigration introducing, very early, ethnic and cultural diversity. The earliest appear to have been Negritos, probably unrelated to Java Man or *homo soloensis*, who possessed a Stone Age culture. The next immigrants, and it is not known with any certainty when they came, are referred to as the Veddoids or Dravidians, possibly from Ceylon. The next wave, in all likelihood much larger, called the Proto-Malays, came to the islands via the Malay Peninsula. They easily forded the rivers and lakes that crisscrossed the land now forming the bottom of the shallow Java Sea and Malay Straits. These people settled along the coastal plains of Sumatra, Java, Borneo (Kalimantan), Celebes (Sulawesi) and the other larger islands, driving the Negritos and Veddoids up into the mountain jungles. Considerably later, probably in the millennium before Christ, a second wave of Mongoloid peoples swept southward from Central Asia and Southwest China. This group, usually called the Deutero-Malays, possessed a more advanced culture in agriculture, warfare and so on and easily drove the coastal inhabitants into the hills, taking for themselves the richer coastal plains, which were soon transformed into paddy fields. Wet rice cultivation thus provided the economic base for the development of a more advanced culture and society. In contemporary Indonesia, the Javanese, Sundanese, Balinese and Malays are descendants of the Deutero-Malay immigrants. The Bataks, Dyaks (or Dajaks) and Toradjas are groups that developed out of the Proto-Malay wave. In view of the natural barriers to communication between these peoples—the steep mountains, dense jungles, wide seas and primitive means of travel—it is not difficult to understand why such a pronounced degree of cultural distinctiveness developed. But this is only part of the picture; more diverse and insistent influences were yet to come.

From India came the first outside influences on the peoples inhabiting the archipelago. Under conditions not yet well understood, early in the Christian era there was a movement of Indian cultural elements, notably religious and ceremonial, into the western half of the Indies. By the eighth century, Hinduism and Buddhism, together with the literary and moral traditions of the *Ramayana, Mahabharata* and other sacred books of India, had become deeply rooted in the life of the common people as well as of the political elite. The syncretistic amalgam of the new religions with the religiously dominated indigenous cultures of Sumatra and Java provided the spiritual basis for extensive and powerful empires: the kingdoms of Shailendra and Srivijaya in Java and Sumatra from the seventh to the eleventh centuries, and of Singhasari, Mataram and Madjapahit on Java from the tenth to the seventeenth centuries. The societies that flowered during these centuries produced magnificent cultural monuments in stone, in music, drama, dance and literary forms as well as in moral, mystical and ceremonial systems. Their influence spread widely throughout the western and central islands of the archipelago.

During the same period Chinese traders, pilgrims and explorers came in search of knowledge, empire and economic gain. But because of the narrow interests, exclusiveness and superior attitude that characterized these traders, Chinese culture made far less broad and deep an impact on Indonesian society than did Indian culture.

The eastward expansion of Islam, reaching the Indies in the twelfth century, brought the next major wave of Asian cultural influence. At first the acceptance of Islam was slow and limited. But the appearance of the first Westerners at the end of the fifteenth century facilitated the penetration of Islam, both geographically and culturally, possibly because people hoped that it would inspire resistance to the encroachments of the Portuguese, English and Dutch. Whatever the motives, it is a fact that by the beginning of the seventeenth century, when the Dutch descended on Indonesia, Islam had become firmly implanted from the western tip of Sumatra to the island of Lombok, east of Java, and in the coastal areas of the islands of Borneo, Celebes and the northern Moluccas. In some cases the Prophet was fanatically revered, as in Atjeh, Menangkabau, Pasundan, West Java, Madura and South Sulawesi. In other areas Islam was held more lightly, like a veneer on the traditional culture, as in Central and East Java. Some rejected it completely, such as the mountain tribes in North Sumatra, Central Sulawesi and Bali. But everywhere in Indonesia, whether held fanatically or tolerantly, Muslim faith and practice took seriously the culture and religion of the people, compromising itself in many respects, particularly by accommodating to customary law or *adat*.

The coming of Islam resulted in Hinduism, as a distinct religion, being forced out of Java and over to Bali, where it became deeply fused with the indigenous Balinese religion. Today, the Hindu-Bali religion is embraced by nearly all Balinese and has given a unique character to social and cultural life.

The next substantial cultural influence penetrating Indonesia came from the West. Since the beginning of the sixteenth century when the first European traders appeared, Western cultural influences have made an impact of steadily increasing breadth and depth. First the Portuguese established a foothold and attempted to secure a monopoly on the fabulously profitable spice trade. The English were always formidable competitors, but it was the Dutch who finally supplanted the Portuguese at the opening of the seventeenth century. English influence was pronounced for a short time during the Napoleonic wars, when English power replaced the Dutch from 1811 to 1816. It was primarily through the Dutch that the peoples of Indonesia felt the influences of the West. Those influences became more focused and universally applied when a colonial administration responsible to the Crown and Parliament succeeded the Dutch East India Company in 1799. Until then Dutch efforts, carried out through "the Company," were primarily commercial and military, the latter to support the former. The goal was to secure products of the Indies highly valued on the European market, such as nutmeg, cloves, peppers, and sandal-wood, in order to gain a monopoly on this trade and thus maintain a fantastically high profit margin. The wars fought by Dutch naval forces against the Spanish and Portuguese, the English, and various Indonesian princes were undertaken to achieve this goal. This policy, however, did not involve much direct interference in the domestic affairs of Indonesian societies, so long as the required amount of produce was forthcoming.

Following 1815 the pattern changed, especially on the island of Java, where thereafter the Dutch concentrated their efforts. The controlled production of agricultural commodities under van den Bosch's "culture system" (1830–1870), the "reforms" under the Liberal government (1870–1900), the "ethical policy" (1900–1930), and the disastrous effects of the general depression (1929–1936) on economic and social conditions in Indonesia all exerted profoundly disturbing influences on Indonesia's diverse societies and cultures.

Other elements in the diversity of Indonesia today, which have only appeared since Independence, are the influences emanating from post-World War II Asia and the United Nations. One need only recall the Afro-Asian Conference in 1955 in Bandung, West Java, and reflect on the *Pantja Sila* principles affirmed as a basis for relations between African and Asian nations and the influence of Chou En-Lai and Nehru in that conference, to be aware of the effect of the two giant neighbors—India to the west and China to the north—on Indonesia. All three of these great Asian nations are experiencing the gargantuan problems involved in achieving unity, stability and development after experiencing subjection and humiliation under the imperialism of Western nations in Asia.

The United Nations too, through Indonesia's active participation (except for 1965), especially in the International Monetary Fund and the International Bank for Reconstruction and Development, is exerting significant influences on developing Indonesia. These influences are truly international and are therefore more easily acceptable to Indonesians than bilateral forms of cooperation that reflect conflicting national interests.

The Economic Foundation

Out of this land, people, history and culture a modern economy is being built. Careful consideration of the two key structural aspects of that economy—island fragmentation and technological dualism—are necessary to an understanding of Indonesia's present plight.

The first characteristic, island fragmentation, is closely related to the geographic and human resources already discussed. It is also, however, partly a result of the economic policies of the colonial government, particularly during the last century. The economy developed by the colonial power was not balanced and integrated to serve the needs and interests of the populace on all the various islands. These were therefore not coordinated in a national economic community. Instead, a geographic dualism developed between Java and the outer provinces. In both areas are to be found two types of production: that geared to meeting the immediate needs of the population, and that oriented to international commerce. On Java, where especially between 1830 and 1870 population grew dense, crowding the limited land, food production and domestic consumer manufactures dominated the economic field. On the outer islands (Sumatra, Kalimantan, Sulawesi and East Indonesia), where population was sparse and land more plentiful, economic activities were oriented toward plantation and small-holder production of agricultural commodities (such as rubber, coffee, copra, spices) for the export trade. It was in the outer islands, too, where extractive industries to exploit mineral resources were most vigorously developed.

This pattern remained basically unchanged after Independence, with the result that economic activity on each of the major islands continues to be oriented more toward the economy of that island itself and outward to foreign countries than toward national interisland markets. Political independence in 1949 was not accompanied by economic independence; rather the colonial pattern of the economy, with control vested in Western or Chinese hands, continued intact for at least a decade.

The second major structural characteristic of the Indonesian economy is technological dualism. There are two distinctive contrasting sectors. The traditional sector, whether in the agricultural or the home industry sphere, is indigenous labor-intensive with a minimum of capital investment. It is dominated by ethnic Indonesians and exists on all the islands.

In contrast is the modern sector, which is capital-intensive and operates in plantation agriculture, mining and industry and also in transport, communications and public utilities. Because of the heavy demand for capital, it has been dominated by foreign interests, which alone could supply the investment capital. Consequently this sector of the economy, during the colonial period at least, made little contribution to the Indonesian economy. The distributive system also operated, at least until 1960, largely under the control and for the profit of Europeans and Chinese.

This pronounced dualism in the Indonesian economy had important consequences, which are still operative despite the fact that since the late 1950's government intervention in the economy has sought to mitigate the effects of alien control. In the first place there developed steadily widening disparities in per capita income in the two sectors. The figures for 1930 in the following table[1] reveal clearly the degree to which Indonesians, especially the Javanese, were excluded from the modern, capital-intensive part of the economy and from receiving a share in its profits.

Group	Java and Madura	Outer Islands	Average for Indonesia
Ethnic Indonesians	55 guilders	66 guilders	59 guilders
Nonethnic Indonesians	310 guilders	320 guilders	310 guilders
Europeans	2,300 guilders	3,200 guilders	2,500 guilders

These disparities in income certainly continued at least through 1958. Most of the available government capital has been used to Indonesianize the distributive, banking and transport facilities. Nevertheless, it was estimated recently that around 80 percent of the distributive system is still in the hands of nonethnic Indonesians.

In the second place, technological dualism, involving as it does foreign control over much of the modern sector, has "hampered the Westernization of the traditional sector by reducing the possibilities for the transmission to it of attitudes that might induce capital formation, a lowered birth rate and other fundamental changes related to growth."[2] The population dynamics have tended to perpetuate this technological dualism and stagnation in the labor-intensive sector by eating up capital formation. The following table, which shows the situation in 1962, gives an idea of the relative size of these two sectors.[3]

Sector Production	Percent Labor-Intensive	Percent Capital-Intensive	Percent of Total Value
Agriculture	94.7	5.3	56.6
Nonagriculture	52.0	48.0	43.4
Total	76.1	23.9	100.0

Thus the agricultural sector of the economy accounted for 56.6 percent of the total production, while the modern, capital-intensive sector accounted for only about 24 percent of the total. It is doubtful whether developments since 1958 have substantially altered the situation, except to further emphasize the agricultural, labor-intensive sector, as government economic policies have depressed the modern sector.

Thus it does not appear that the structural weaknesses and limitations inherent in island fragmentation and technological dualism have as yet been substantially changed as a result of Independence.

FOOTNOTES
1. Douglas Paauw, "From Colonial to Guided Economy," in R. McVey (ed.), *Indonesia*. New Haven: Human Relations Area Files Press, 1963, p. 173.
2. *Ibid.*, p. 172.
3. *Ibid.*, p. 174.

2 Indonesia's Postcolonial Revolution

RECENT INDONESIAN DEVELOPMENTS HAVE baffled observers. Those concerned primarily with the political situation saw a Communist take-over as virtually assured after the direction of guided democracy emerged clearly in the early 1960's. Yet recent events have shown dramatically that a Communist victory is farther from realization than at any time since 1949. Again, commentators on the economic situation have prophesied imminent collapse since the late 1950's. Yet while severe economic malaise can be demonstrated by any measure, economic collapse has not occurred. These failures in prediction are due partly to inadequate knowledge and understanding of Indonesian society. They also suggest, perhaps, that measures, concepts and models commonly employed in the West may have limited applicability for comprehending the Indonesian reality.

Here, then, is an attempt to picture the present state of Indonesian society against the background of the colonial past. What is happening in Indonesia today is revolution—radical and rapid change in all spheres of life, not just in politics and government. This revolutionary change is inseparably connected with the colonial subjugation experienced by the Indonesian people. It is a postcolonial revolution, and therefore is not to be understood as similar to the revolutions in the West in the eighteenth and nineteenth centuries. Out of the Westerner's experience with revolution in his own past, and because of his participation in the colonial domination of Asia and Africa, he does not hear what Asians are saying when they talk about their revolutions, nor does he seem to comprehend the realities of the Asian revolution today. For the Westerner and the Asian are on the opposite ends of colonialism.

Though the social and cultural are undoubtedly the most basic and determinative dimensions of the Indonesian revolution, it is perhaps easiest to get at them through the political and economic forces that came with colonialism and largely forced and fashioned the social and cultural change. Thus the political and economic dimensions of the revolution will be treated before the social and cultural.

The Political Revolution

Indonesia was not a nation before the arrival of Western power in the late fifteenth century. It consisted rather of a number of autonomous, indigenous political units in various parts of the archipelago, some relatively large, others quite small. Several times in preceding centuries there had been impressive empires, such as Srividjaya and Madjapahit, which ruled what is present-day Indonesia, except for the three eastern provinces.

Nor did Dutch colonial rule weld the Indonesian peoples into a nation. Unity was emphatically not its goal. On the contrary, until the end it could conceive of Indonesia only as a colony to which was applied the classic colonial principle of "divide and rule." First the Netherlands East India Company (1605–1799) and later the colonial government (1815–1941) followed the practice of indirect rule, that is, the traditional ruling class was maintained to exercise administrative control under the direction of Dutch officials responsible to the Governor General. In this way a relatively small number of colonial administrators were able to carry out their policies more or less effectively through an Indonesian bureaucracy. These Indonesian functionaries, while serving the interests of the colonial government, also served their own interests, sometimes handsomely. The Dutch did not attempt to interfere in the daily life of Indonesians more broadly than was necessary to achieve their economic and political ends. Nor were they too concerned about how the local rulers governed, as long as their ends were served without abuses flagrant enough to arouse rebellion among the people.

This pattern of colonial rule had two aspects that are important to our analysis. First, responsibility was wholly in the hands of the Dutch. The Indonesian functionaries could not determine policy; they could only carry it out under close supervision. Second, little if any political activity among the people was permitted, and none at all was encouraged. The political associations that began to develop after the turn of the century did not have any legitimate range of activity. And the few Indonesians who sat in the Governor General's Advisory Council (Volksraad) after 1925 were appointed rather than elected.

Dutch rule ended in 1941 without having given Indonesians any appreciable political or governmental experience. More significantly, only a handful of Indonesians from the upper class were given the opportunity to pursue higher education, and they were limited to the fields of medicine, engineering and law.

During the Japanese occupation Indonesians gained considerable political and administrative experience through both legitimate and underground activities. As the Pacific war progressed and the outcome became clearer, nationalist leaders, headed by Sukarno and Hatta, were permitted more freedom to organize and were encouraged by the Japanese to prepare for Independence. It is doubtful that Independence would have come as soon as it did had not the Japanese occupation eliminated the Dutch for a time and provided the nationalist movement both stimulus to grow and opportunity to gain experience.

Independence was proclaimed by Sukarno and Hatta on August 17, 1945, two days after the cease-fire in the Pacific war. This proclamation, however, was not respected by the Dutch who, with the help of the Allies, returned to establish their colonial rule over Indonesia. Thus the first four and one-half years of Independence (August, 1945 to December, 1949) were spent under a temporary constitution and under alternating conditions of physical conflict and negotiations with the Dutch. During this first period of Indonesian Independence, in which the Republican government's control did not extend beyond some parts of Java and Sumatra, the Basic Constitution of 1945 provided for a presidential Cabinet. Various political parties were already active, notably Nationalist, Communist and Islamic parties, and some of the interparty conflicts, which were to become common in the next period, appeared. While fighting for its life against the Dutch, the Indonesian government also managed to quell a Communist insurrection at Madiun in 1948.

Thus, this first phase of Indonesian Independence was physical revolution. The new government was forced to fight not only against the Dutch for the Independence it had proclaimed against them, but also against its own Communist party to defend its sovereignty. Another dimension of political revolution is to be seen in the largely spontaneous and sometimes violent acts of repudiation by the populace, for example in Atjeh, of the traditional ruling class, which had collaborated with the Dutch colonial government. The new political elite tended to come from the younger grouping of students and the military and civil bureaucracy, who took an active part in the struggle for Independence against both the Japanese and the Dutch. Finally, during this period new political structures and procedures were being constructed. A more detailed constitution, the Provisional Constitution of 1950, was drawn up to serve until a Constitutional Assembly could be elected and draft a permanent Constitution.

The second period began after the Dutch, under strong United Nations pressure, granted Indonesians their sovereignty on December 27, 1949. This period, from 1950 through 1958, is often designated the period of liberal parliamentary democracy. The Provisional Constitution of 1950 provided for a Cabinet responsible to the Parliament and headed by a Prime Minister. Members of Parliament represented the dozens of political parties, which are generally classifiable as nationalist, Marxist or religious. Because the three or four larger parties were relatively equally balanced and there were many smaller parties, government was always an unstable coalition arrangement. Between 1950 and 1959, when guided democracy was instituted, there were nine cabinets. President Sukarno, who had played a dominant front and center role in the first period under the short-lived Constitution of 1945, was now head of state and yielded the stage to the party leaders who rose and fell with the rapid succession of cabinets. Nevertheless, Sukarno played a skillful and powerful behind-the-scenes role, which was often decisive.

During this period three rebellions broke out: the Republic of South Moluccas affair in 1950-1952; the Darul Islam rebellion in West Java and Central Sulawesi, which continued throughout the period; and the rebellion in Sumatra and Northern Sulawesi, which lasted from 1958 to 1962. These rebellions took a heavy toll in lives, property and government expenditure. They reflected dissatisfaction on the part of the regions with the central government, in which economic, religious and ethnic considerations all played a role.

Still another event reflected the continuing political revolution. The year after the general elections in 1955, which gave Indonesia its first elected Parliament, elections were held for a Constitutional Assembly to draft a permanent Constitution for Indonesia. Several years of work served to settle only such minor matters as the national anthem and the national flag. On the question of the basis of the state, there was sharp conflict between the Muslim parties and the others, the former urging an Islamic state based on the Koran, and the latter holding out for a secular state based on the Pantja Sila, or Five Principles: Belief in God, Nationalism, Humanitarianism (sometimes called Internationalism), the People's Sovereignty and Social Justice. Debate over this key issue became so heated toward the end of 1958 that President Sukarno, already faced with rebellion in Sumatra and North Sulawesi and fearing full-scale civil war, used his presidential powers to adjourn the Constitutional Assembly.

His action was a first formal step in instituting the new political system, guided democracy, which was formally decreed by President Sukarno in July, 1959. It was a return to the simple Constitution of 1945, which provided for a Cabinet responsible to the President, a Parliament in which elected members were supplemented by presidentially appointed members, and a Provisional Peoples' Consultative Council, appointed by the President and vested with power to determine general direction and policy of the state. The President carried the mandate of this body and assumed the office of Prime Minister, his Cabinet being led by several Deputy Prime Ministers.

This third period in the political revolution of Indonesia lasted from July, 1959, to March, 1966. The five basic elements that theoretically characterized it, expressed in the acronym USDEK, were: the 1945 Constitution, Indonesian Socialism, Guided Democracy, Guided Economy and the Indonesian Identity. But in reality there was only one element behind all these terms—the leadership of Sukarno, who over the period assumed a long string of titles. The following were the most important: President for Life, Great Leader of the Revolution, Commander-in-Chief of the Armed Forces, Mandate Holder of the Provisional Peoples' Consultative Conference, and Prime Minister. He formed the cabinets, dominated the various councils of state, determined the main lines of both domestic and foreign policy, simplified the party system by cutting the number to ten and generally controlled these parties through his lieutenants. He was in fact the leader of this phase of the revolution. He was the one person ultimately responsible for the successful campaign to regain Indonesian sovereignty over Irian Barat (West New Guinea); for the increasing alignment of Indonesia with the policies of the Peoples' Republic of China; for the unsuccessful "confrontation" with Malaysia; for the withdrawal of

Indonesia from the United Nations and its international agencies in January, 1965; and for the advanced deterioration of the nation's economic condition.

Sukarno's method of dominating the national scene was a mixture of propaganda and indoctrination on the one hand, and clever political in-fighting and maneuvering on the other. He managed to secure the allegiance of, or at least prevail over the leadership of, the three dominant political groups—the Communist, Nationalist and Muslim Scholars parties—and of the Armed Forces; and he also kept a measure of balance among them. For a time he seemed to be succeeding in blending the three main sources of ideas and motivation for the Indonesian revolution—nationalism, religion and communism—into an alliance, or at least into a working relationship (symbolized by NASAKOM). But this turned out to be the reef on which he ran his ship aground. Many place directly on him responsibility for the tragic events of 1965-66, which brought to an end the period of guided democracy he dominated. In an indirect sense, at least, he was responsible. For it is clear that in the violent reaction of the Indonesian people to the attempted coup of October 1, 1965 (in which hundreds of thousands of people were killed, many of them alleged Communist activists or sympathizers) Sukarno's leadership was repudiated. In the violence of that event, and in the radical shift that ultimately succeeded it, are revealed the depth and unpredictability (and at times uncontrollability) of the revolutionary forces that built up and were unleashed during the period of Sukarno's guided democracy.

In March, 1966, when governmental authority was transferred by President Sukarno to General Suharto, the Army Commander who had frustrated the attempted coup, a new phase of the Indonesian revolution began. In June, the Provisional Peoples' Consultative Council directed the new Cabinet: first, to give top priority to economic stabilization and rehabilitation; second, to restore an active and independent foreign policy; and third, to prepare for general elections in 1968. The Cabinet has already made significant progress on this program, by first bringing to a conclusion the "confrontation" with Malaysia, then leading Indonesia back into the United Nations and its related international agencies and, perhaps most significantly, preparing a vigorous attack on the economic stagnation that had steadily grown worse under Sukarno's leadership.

Clearly the political revolution in Indonesia is still in full course. Political institutions continue to be in flux. The years since 1945 have provided experience, if at times bitter, out of which can be expected to evolve a more stable political and governmental system. How long this process will take cannot be predicted, partly because it depends on other dimensions of the Indonesian revolution.

The Economic Dimension

Before the coming of the Westerner, Indonesia had a subsistence agricultural economy with barter as the only form of exchange, even for the spices and other commodities sought by foreign traders. Early European economic penetration in the sixteenth through the eighteenth centuries consisted primarily of trade, along with necessary incentives and controls. It was almost monopolized by the Dutch East India Company. Early in the nineteenth century, when the Indies were returned by the British to the Dutch after the Napoleonic wars, a much more vigorous policy of economic penetration was undertaken by the colonial powers to stimulate cash crop production of agricultural commodities for the European market. This involved the expansion of a money economy, the large-scale leasing of agricultural lands of the people for estates cultivating tea, coffee, rubber, sugar, tobacco, and other profitable items.

Transportation and communication—roads, railways and shipping lines—joined islands and regions, facilitating the movement of peoples. Cities grew, and urbanization became a problem. New economic institutions sprang up, especially in the cities, opening new opportunities to Indonesians. Western ways of life became more common. The economic and material aspirations of the people rose much more rapidly than the available means to satisfy them. Economic development was oriented primarily to the export-import sphere. It was controlled by foreign interests both European and alien Asian, and the livelihood of the great majority was neglected. These characteristics made the total Indonesian economy potentially vulnerable and actually weak. This fact became cruelly evident in the years between 1929 and 1939, when the effects of world depression brought great suffering to the Indonesian people. Incidentally, it was only during these years that any consumer industry to speak of developed in Indonesia, and then only in beginning stages.

During the Japanese occupation access to Europe was cut off. Though subjected to extreme demands of the occupying power the economy began to move toward balance, as both agricultural and industrial production was emphasized.

It is necessary to examine in somewhat more detail the performance of the Indonesian economy during the turbulent period since sovereignty was assured in 1949. Various measures are used by economists to evaluate the performance of a particular national economy. But all agree that what happens to the cost of living is a significant reflection of the state of the economy. The cost of living index for Indonesia from 1951 to the middle of 1966 shows that in those years—most of the period of Indonesian political sovereignty—the cost of living has increased 1,700 times, or 170,355 percent. It is equally important to recognize that there has been a sharply accelerating rate of annual increase in the cost of living: averaging 10 percent for 1951-1953, 20 percent for 1954-1957, 40 percent for 1958-1960, 205 percent for 1961-1965, and a skyrocketing 634 percent for 1966. This condition was accurately described in October, 1966, by the Presidium Minister for Economic and Financial Affairs, as "raging inflation."

Several facts should be noted from the data on state expenditures, revenues and budget deficits for the period. First, while the real income of Indonesia increased from 306 billion *rupiahs* in 1951 to 430 billion in 1965, or slightly over 40 percent, the population increased from approximately 75 to 109 million, or roughly 45 percent. This means that per capita income dropped 5 percent over 14 years, or between 0.3 percent and 0.4 percent per year. According to Dr. Emil Salim, the per capita income decreased 0.7 percent per year between 1958 and 1965. This fact suggests that in the years since 1960, the people's standard of living has been falling at an accelerating rate because of the growing disparity between the rate of economic growth and the rate of population growth.

Second, the rate of inflation reflected in the difference between the nominal and corrected figures for net national income is startling. Third, state expenditures composed between 10 and 15 percent of the national income between 1951 and 1960, but dropped to 4 percent by 1965 and were still lower the following year. State revenues reflect the same tendency, which means that through 1966 the government's budget had been assuming a steadily and sharply decreasing role in the net national income.

In sharp contrast, however, the budget deficit shows precisely the opposite trend. This suggests one of the main reasons for inflation and the steadily rising cost of living index. During these years, especially since 1958, the government met the budget deficits by issuing new money and expanding bank credit to government agencies and enterprises. An examination of the relevant data reveals that this has resulted in a corresponding swelling of the amount and velocity of money in circulation. As commodities became increasingly scarce and inflation steeper, people were less and less inclined to hold on to cash. Therefore, increased velocity of circulation built up as money ever more intensely sought goods.

There is another factor in the economic equation, the relation of imports and exports; for these concern the supply of goods and services, the very stuff of economic activity. A study of the performance of the export-import sector of the Indonesian economy over the period under consideration shows that, with the exception of mineral produc,ucts, especially petroleum, the volume of exports dropped steadily by more than 50 percent between 1939 and 1962. The increase in petroleum exports, however, was such that the total export volume was up by 17 percent for the same period. The figures on foreign exchange earnings from exports show that the decrease in value of exports continued steadily right up to 1965.

The pattern of exports also changed between 1939 and 1962. In volume of export, minerals increased from 62 percent to 88 percent of the total, while vegetable items decreased from 38 percent to 12 percent of the total. Measured by the value of export commodities, rubber's share grew from 28 percent to 44 percent of the total, and petroleum products from 20 percent to 32 percent. All other exports dropped from 48 percent to 25 percent of the total. This picture is not an encouraging one as far as diversification of the economy is concerned. In 1962, 75.5 percent of Indonesia's foreign exchange was earned on only two items, rubber and petroleum.

The various factors accounting for this relative drop in exports cannot be discussed here. Yet whatever the reasons, a drop in export earnings of over 50 percent between 1951 and 1965 must adversely affect the economy of a nation whose population increased more than 45 percent during the same period. It means that all categories of imports—consumer goods, raw materials and capital goods—had to be kept far below the level required for economic growth, unless these imports could be financed by foreign loans.

During the same period, in fact, Indonesia incurred foreign obligations—short- and long-term loans, deferred payment agreements and credits—totaling nearly $2.5 billion, a staggering amount for the size of the Indonesian economy. This could have served to stimulate economic growth if correctly used. A major portion, however, was invested not in productive enterprise but in military equipment and in prestige construction. A portion was invested in development projects, but these either have not yet been completed or have not had time to produce results in the economy.

A close examination of the yearly level of imports shows marked variation from year to year, especially between 1955 and 1962. Such instability reflects, among other things, the erratic application of fiscal policies and monetary controls to the field of exports and imports. This in turn reflects in part the political instability that rendered both the formulation of and adherence to coherent and comprehensive rational economic policies extremely difficult, if not impossible.

During the years 1951–1962 a decline of more than 30 percent in export earnings was matched by an increase of 88 percent in volume of imports. From 1961 to 1965, when exports fell still further, by more than 33 percent, the level of imports was relatively steady, at an average of $230 million per year. But this figure is far too low, only a third of what is needed to keep industry operating at near capacity, not to mention the import of essential consumption commodities and capital goods for rehabilitation and development. Thus, the years 1951 to 1965 witnessed a steady deterioration in the Indonesian economy. The flow of money (*rupiahs*) increased rapidly, while the flow of goods fell markedly. The longer this trend continued and the farther it developed, the more difficult it became to slow or reverse it, except by radical action.

The political explosion, which burst on October 1 in the form of an abortive coup d'etat, eventuated in another radical change in leadership and direction of the Indonesian revolution. The era of guided democracy with its guided economy appeared to have ended. The Sultan of Jogjakarta, now Presidium Minister for Economic and Financial Affairs of Indonesia, looking back on this period, said in an address on October 3, 1966:

> For the last seven years the economy of Indonesia has been steadily deteriorating at an increasingly rapid pace, bringing along abysmal discrepancies between the incomes of the different groups in our country. Figures will show you the increase of the price level, the decrease of exports, the decrease of government revenues, the increased money in circulation and so on, but the laborers, civil servants, members of the Armed Forces, in short all people with fixed incomes will tell you, if you will be able to listen to them, of the daily hardships, the impossibility of making both ends meet, the great shortage of medicines and all those things which represent our minimum demands in life.

Between January and July, 1966, the cost of living increased more than four times; during the same period of time, the total money supply increased from 2,750 to 10,000 billion *rupiahs,* or 3.6 times, while the foreign exchange earnings from exports fell slightly, as against a doubled rate of necessary imports. Thus the new government established in July, 1966, inherited an economy that is "in a deplorable state," as one of the three top leaders put it recently. The flow of money was increasing rapidly in both volume and speed, while the flow of commodities slowed, as imports dropped and domestic industry produced at less than 30 percent of capacity. Per capita income in 1966 dropped at a rate probably in excess of one percent for the year. The Minister of Labor, speaking in Pakanbaru, Riau, in October, 1966, stated that there were three million unemployed people and 10 million underemployed in a total labor market of 38.5 million. Thus with 1.3 million new jobs needing to be found each year, the economy has to support 8 percent unemployment and 26 percent underemployment, while the total work force amounts to only 54.1 percent of the population 10 years of age and older. There is revealed on the one hand a picture of skyrocketing inflation, on the other of almost complete stagnation.

Most recent estimates predict foreign exchange earnings for 1966 at slightly over $500 million, with that figure rising to perhaps $600 million by 1968. But during these same years Indonesia's scheduled repayment of foreign obligations of roughly $2.2 billion calls for $530 million in 1966, $269 million in 1967 and $274 million in 1968. This is a situation of near bankruptcy on the international scale. There seems to be little hope for an early substantial increase of imports, which is needed to bring the flow of goods into better balance with the flow of money.

This situation became clear to the new leaders shortly after their appointment in March, 1966. The nation's top economists produced a diagnosis and prognosis, which became the basis of Decision XXXIII of the 1966 Provisional People's Consultative Council on "The Renovation of Economic, Financial and Developmental Policies." That decision gave a mandate to the new cabinet to make an immediate and forthright attack on the economic stagnation by formulating the basic principles and policies for a program of economic rehabilitation and stabilization. But time is short, for the new political stability achieved in recent months can only be maintained if positive progress is registered in achieving economic stability.

Certain conclusions can be drawn from this description of the present state of the Indonesian economy. First, there appears to be a basis for cautious optimism that positive progress may be made in bringing relief to the long-suffering Indonesian people's economic distress. The new government manifests an adequate grasp of the nature and causes of the economic crisis and knows the steps that must be taken toward solution. Both its efforts at analysis and the adoption of realistic measures have been considerably reinforced by its request for help from, and close cooperation with, International Monetary Fund and International Bank for Reconstruction and Development teams. Those efforts have been accompanied by other successful initiatives in rescheduling the repayment of foreign obligations and securing new stop-gap credits needed to launch the rehabilitation program. These developments, however, have to be assessed in light of the continuing uncertainty as to whether the new leadership has achieved sufficient control over the political, social and cultural variables that are intimately related to overall economic development.

While it seems realistic to expect improvement in Indonesia's economic situation, all indicators suggest that it will not be either quick or massive. The present leadership is realistic, but whether the demands and expectations of the Indonesian people can be kept under the discipline of reality and whether their response can be fired with the degree of effort and sacrifice necessary to register advance remains to be demonstrated.

This uncertainty becomes more pertinent in light of a second conclusion. Efforts to control inflation, balance the state budget and stimulate exports will require a more realistic conversion rate with the world's hard currencies. The real cost of living will rise for a time, and therefore the government will have to call on the people for continuing sacrifice. Again, it is realistic to hope for success, *if* the government can demonstrate by its performance that the situation has changed and improvement, even though very slight, is taking place. For persons and programs whose operations in Indonesia have been financed by hard currency, including overseas church agencies, the period ahead will almost certainly bring increased costs for maintenance of personnel, prosecution of programs and especially construction of facilities. Building costs can be expected to increase sharply within the next few years.

Third, substantial foreign assistance will continue to be required in the years immediately ahead, both to increase the volume of goods on the market and to finance import of raw materials, spare parts and new equipment not yet producible in Indonesia. There is general agreement, both in Indonesia and among foreign creditors, that this aid should be multinational in source and multilateral in administration. United States government officials have indicated that this is the direction State Department policy will take, rather than the reestablishment of a large bilateral AID operation in Indonesia. The fruits of experience in Indonesia and elsewhere in Southeast Asia may lead to a more realistic awareness of the limitations of external aid and the institution of trade policies that provide maximum opportunity for nations such as Indonesia to strengthen their powers of indigenous development.

Two additional conclusions relate more directly to patterns of ecumenical cooperation in Indonesia. First, in light of the more rational approach to Indonesia's economic problems reflected in the new government's measures, the interchurch aid efforts supported by Church World Service must, beginning now, place much more emphasis on basic, longer-term economic development programs and projects, particularly in food production and family planning. In some areas, because of the nature of the church and its constituency, the most relevant and practicable beginning of a solid contribution to Indonesia's efforts is to guarantee material well-being for all her people. Very little has been done by the churches on either of these fronts to date, and what has been attempted has by no means produced satisfactory results. Much more serious attention can and should be given to this dimension of the interchurch aid program in Indonesia, though continuing programs designed to meet emergency needs should not be ruled out.

Finally, the churches in Indonesia have repeatedly acknowledged responsibility for participating critically, creatively and enthusiastically in the economic, social and cultural dimensions of the Indonesian revolution. Here is one of the most critical challenges for a church that feels called to make a contribution to nation building. Nor should the church enter this arena, especially in postcolonial Indonesia, under the illusion that it has a time-tested, doctrinaire answer to offer. Especially in the economic sphere the Christian church has failed, notably in the "Christian" West, to bring the resources of its faith to bear on the problems of people's economic welfare. A new opportunity confronts the churches in Indonesia, but also a critical challenge that demands full utilization, first of all and above all, of the intellectual and spiritual resources with which the worldwide Christian community has been endowed and of which it needs to become aware.

The Social-Cultural Dimension

Beneath the surface waves of revolution in the political and economic spheres flow the deeper social and cultural currents. Whenever political and economic aspects are analyzed, it becomes evident that social-cultural forces more or less determine possibilities for change in those spheres. For example, economic rehabilitation will require a new discipline of work, a new pattern of values and incentives, a more efficient administrative structure, more effective controls. Given the present social-cultural situation, what are the chances that the necessary radical economic measures can be taken?

There is little data available on the social and cultural dimensions of the Indonesian revolution, for the specialists have tended to concentrate on political and economic affairs rather than on sociological and anthropological research on contemporary Indonesian society.

Indonesian societies, before the coming of Western influences, were communal in nature, some simple and others complex. Their economic base was agricultural. They were locally oriented, finding most of their interest in the village or immediate surroundings. They were traditional in outlook, with the pattern of leadership predominantly a paternalistic authoritarianism. Wisdom resided with the aged. Life was slow-paced, in keeping with the cyclical rhythm of nature. Major social institutions tended to cluster around the functions of kinship, government and religion, though in a complex communal society such as the Javanese or Menangkabau, economic institutions were also developed. The many ethnic societies in the archipelago remained relatively isolated from one another.

Colonial rule, bringing new political, economic, religious and cultural factors into these established societies, forced drastic changes. For example, Christianity took root and grew in Indonesia alongside Hindu, Buddhist and other religious minorities in a society with an Islamic majority of at least 85 percent. But Christianity has had a social and cultural influence greater than its numbers would suggest.

The Chinese were another minority group created and encouraged by the colonial government. To meet the need for disciplined labor, experienced entrepreneurs and strongly motivated traders, the Dutch encouraged Chinese immigration to facilitate development of the modern sector of the economy. Their achievement of a dominant economic position both encouraged tension between ethnic Indonesians and aliens and handicapped ethnic Indonesians in developing skills in the commercial field. Thus the Chinese minority has enhanced complexity as well as tension and diversity in Indonesian society.

A third effect of colonial rule was the unintended but inevitable multiplying of contacts and relationships among members of diverse ethnic groups within Indonesia. In order to man the Royal Dutch Army and Navy, the civil bureaucracy, the railway and steamship lines, the educational and other institutions, the Dutch recruited personnel from various regions—Ambonese, Bataks, Manadonese, Timorese— transporting them to other parts of Indonesia. Many were sent to Java, greatly hastening the process of social and cultural amalgamation. Naturally this mixing process did not always proceed harmoniously; there was underlying tension much of the time and occasionally open conflict. But a start was made toward the achievement of unity in the midst of diversity.

Another factor introducing change was the increasing number of Indonesians entering the new world of education and technology. Under the colonial government this new elite was kept small, and the door to liberating knowledge and skills was opened only a crack. Nevertheless, this tiny group of intellectuals, made up mostly of sons of the ruling aristocracy or Indo-Europeans, was a symbol of what was to come after Independence.

Finally, during the colonial period there grew up a variety of new associations with political, economic, religious, social and cultural interests, such as Sarekat Islam, Budi Utomo, Nationalist party, Communist party, labor unions, churches, study clubs and the like. These represented a new kind of structure in Indonesian society—the voluntary association—which heralded a significant change from a communal to an associational social organization. The traditional, static, rural, homogeneous, backward-looking character of indigenous Indonesian society was beginning to yield, under the impact of outside influences, to the rational, dynamic, urban, heterogeneous, forward-looking qualities that characterize modern society.

World War I, the Great Depression, the Pacific war and Japanese occupation accelerated the rate and broadened the scope of social change, so that by the time the Indonesian people proclaimed their Independence in 1945 it was obvious that Indonesian society was in full revolution. During the years since Independence, the following main aspects of the social revolution stood out.

First, in the sphere of leadership, members of the Indonesian ruling elite who had discredited themselves in the eyes of the people by collaborating with the Dutch colonial regime were eliminated, if not physically at least from positions of political power. As a result, the most important segment of social leadership had to be replaced. The new leadership personnel was increasingly drawn from the youth, the women, the armed forces, the educational institutions and those active in the political parties. Because of the lack of development of modern economic enterprises under Indonesian control, economic institutions made almost no contribution to the new leadership, and therefore the new leadership was largely without knowledge of or experience in economic enterprise.

To a significant degree a parallel change occurred in the patterns and processes of leadership. Clearly the needs of a newly independent nation could not be served by the patterns established to administer a colonial regime. Yet these were the only patterns and processes known to the new elite. Nor would a return to the indigenous pattern of leadership be either possible or desirable for a people already moving strongly toward a modern society. Hence for the first decade of Independence, no attempt was evident to return to indigenous patterns or to develop new patterns of leadership. Instead a new corps of leaders took over to operate through patterns and processes of leadership inherited from the West, in which, however, they had had relatively little opportunity for training or experience. It soon became evident that in sphere after sphere—in political parties and their mass organizations, in religious bodies, in educational institutions and throughout government, and after 1957 in the nationalized economic enterprises—leadership patterns and processes proved inadequate and crises developed.

Thus in many spheres of Indonesian life since Independence, there has been a search for patterns of leadership, decision-making and administration that can achieve more stability, efficiency and development.

A second revolutionary trend in Indonesian society is the rapid expansion of education. Under the colonial regime education was possible only for the privileged few. The 1930 census revealed a literacy rate of less than 10 percent. Today it is eight times that figure. The educational system has been revised and expanded. Only lack of capital for facilities and time to train an adequate number of teachers stand in the way of a full implementation of the compulsory education law. Especially at the level of higher education, the change has been amazing. In 1940 there was no university in the Dutch East Indies and probably not more than 1,000 Indonesians in institutes above the secondary level. In 1965 there were 179 colleges and universities enrolling about 250,000 students. Consequently, education has assumed an increasingly important role as an agent of social and cultural change in Indonesian society. It is providing resources of knowledge, experience and research that are beginning to fill the gap caused by the neglect of education for Indonesians under colonial rule. The revolutionary power in education was seen in the role played by students in the overthrow of Sukarno's regime in 1966.

Related to both leadership and education is the acceleration in social mobility that has occurred since 1945. A wide field of new opportunity is now open to Indonesians in political and economic fields, in education and in the armed forces. While many positions of leadership continue to be filled by those originating from the ruling classes, opportunities for those from other classes are more widely available now. This is particularly true in the armed forces, which have come to play a leading role in Indonesian society in the past 10 years, and especially since the attempted coup. They hold, together with the intelligentsia, the key to future developments in Indonesia.

A final aspect of revolutionary social change is social controls. There has hardly been a year since the establishment of the Republic in which Indonesian society has been free of major acts of violence. Most of these have been referred to already: the struggle against the Dutch, 1945-1949; the Communist rebellion in 1948; the Republic of South Moluccas rebellion, 1950-1952; the Darul-Islam rebellion, which flared sporadically from 1950 to 1964; the PRRI-PERMESTA Rebellion, 1958-1960; the struggle for West Irian, 1961-1963; the confrontation against Malaysia along the North Kalimantan border, 1963-1965; and the savage aftermath of the October 1 coup, which lasted well into 1966. In addition, armed bandits have victimized the people in such areas as West and Central Java, South Sulawesi and North Sumatra. There have been riots and violence against minority groups, notably the Chinese, at various times and places. The legacy of colonialism and resistance against the Japanese, the waxing tides of nationalism, and the repeated campaigns against colonialism and imperialism, the struggle to the death between the religious and Communist parties, the radical politicizing of all spheres of life, including the attempt to revise existing legal codes and procedure during the guided democracy period, and the steadily worsening standard of living for a large portion of the people have all combined to weaken to the point of total breakdown the traditional system of social control. These same forces have also hindered the development of a new social discipline and cohesion.

These same factors are clearly part of the cultural revolution, which is manifest in the political, social and economic realms. They reflect wide, deep and rapid changes in the norms, values, ideals, expectations, attitudes and spirit that fill the heart, mind and emotions of Indonesian people. The impact of Western culture, through colonialism, and since Independence in circumstances of the cold war and the space age, has been profoundly confusing and disturbing. The traditional world view and ways of thinking and living have been burst open. The community has been immensely enlarged, and this means the enlargement of loyalties and attitudes. New philosophies, ideologies, aesthetic patterns, systems of belief have been introduced, along with science and technology, challenging the simpler, more static and homogeneous cultural patterns. The older generation, which received its orientation during the colonial period, is far removed from the 1945 generation, which grew up in the years of war and revolution. And there will undoubtedly be an even wider culture gap between them and their children, "the 1966 generation."

In summary, Indonesia today is in the full tide of a revolutionary change, of which political independence and the struggle to establish stable yet flexible political and economic institutions is but one manifestation. The same factors that caused it—the aggressive, disruptive influences from an expanding West—have also brought the radical change that characterizes equally, if not more profoundly, the social and cultural spheres. Social groupings (elites, classes, functional groups) and social institutions (based on kinship, government, economic, aesthetic and religious functions) are undergoing rapid change. So are the norms, values, ideas, expectations, attitudes and spirit that constitute the world view and life view of the Indonesian people. What has been happening is a process of transformation of the societies and cultures making up the nation from a traditional to a rational, a rural to an urban, a static to a dynamic, a homogeneous to a heterogeneous, a communal to an associational character. In other words, modernization.

To experience modernization in a society where the political and economic institutions are relatively stable is one thing. But it is altogether different when social and cultural transformation of such radical scope and velocity occur in a society that on the one hand is not yet used to accepting change, and on the other is threatened with chaos in the political and economic realms. In the process of aban-

doning the old and building something new and better, which of the
conflicting ideas, values and principles competing for acceptance shall
be embraced? This is a decisive question; but there is no guarantee that
an early, adequate answer will be found.

The details of where the revolution will lead and what it will produce are not foreseeable. One thing is predictable, however. Whatever
it becomes will not be determined primarily by external forces—
political, economic or religious—but by the dynamic forces within
Indonesian society and culture. Outside forces can help or hinder, to
a degree, but they cannot determine what will develop. Now that the
nation is independent, that will depend on the response of the Indonesian people and their leaders to the options presented by the new
situation.

3 The Church in Indonesia

THIS CHAPTER BEGINS THE ACCOUNT OF the church of Jesus Christ in Indonesia by describing in general the full spectrum of the Christian movement.

All One Body We?

Yes and no! The household of God in Indonesia is, we must believe, one in the intent of the Lord. But to the world its splintered character is painfully more evident than its oneness and harmony. Because Islam is the predominant religion, non-Christian Indonesians may be unaware of differences among the various branches of the Christian community and see them as one. But from within, three main categories of Christians are discernible: Roman Catholics, Protestant groups in the Indonesia Council of Churches, and Protestant groups outside the Council.

To distinguish between Roman Catholic and Protestant churches, Indonesians speak of *Geredja Katolik* (the Catholic Church) and *Geredja Kristen* (the Christian Church), the latter meaning Protestant. Protestant Christians number at least three times Roman Catholic believers.

39

Three-fourths of the Protestants are members of the 35 regional churches* that have joined the Council of Churches in Indonesia. This part of the Protestant community, considerably more than 4 million, is distributed among nearly 8,000 congregations located in all the 25 provinces of Indonesia.

The church bodies that have chosen not to cooperate with the Council of Churches or with one another have done so for a variety of reasons. There are at least 20 such bodies and possibly more, since among them are the Pentecostals, who have shown a strong tendency to subdivide. This category of Christians probably numbers somewhat under a million.

The Coming of the Protestant Church

The history of Protestant Christianity in Indonesia falls into four major periods: the period of Portuguese suzerainty 1520–1615; the Dutch East India Company period 1615–1815; the period of activity by foreign missionary societies 1815–1930; and the period of autonomous Indonesian churches since 1930.

In Indonesia as in the West, the Protestant church built on Roman Catholic foundations, which were laid during the period of Portuguese suzerainty. By the end of the sixteenth century, missionary work by the various orders had succeeded in establishing vigorous congregations in the Moluccas, North Sulawesi, Sangir-Talaud islands and on the southeastern islands of Solor, Flores and Timor.

With the victory of the Netherlands East India Company over the Portuguese at the beginning of the seventeenth century, Dutch Reformed Christianity took over most of these congregations. From 1615 to 1815, with the exception of a small Roman Catholic remnant that managed to survive in the isolated southeast region, Christianity in Indonesia came under the control of "the Seventeen Gentlemen" (*De Heeren XVII*) at the Dutch East India Company headquarters in Holland. In short, the church became a "Company church" in the full sense of that term. Dutch ministers were dispatched to serve Company employees in Ambon, Ternate and Banda in the Moluccas, in Batavia, Makassar, Padang, Manado, Semarang and Surabaja. Congregations in the last two cities were established only after 1750. An event of unusual significance for the spread of Christianity in In-

* Three new members were accepted at the Sixth Assembly in November, 1967, bringing the total to 38.

donesia was the publication in 1733 of the first translation of the Bible into the Malay language by Melchior Leydekker. Available statistics indicate clearly that the Company church did little to proclaim the gospel and expand the church. It seemed content to serve the Dutch congregations and give only minimal attention to the Indonesian Christians inherited from the Roman Catholic period.

The third period (1815–1930) began with the return of the Indies by the British to the Dutch in 1816 at the end of the Napoleonic war. What had been a Reformed church under the control and direction of the Netherlands East India Company now became a nondenominational church under the control and direction of the colonial government. Though the official policy, under King William I, was that the government was to be neutral in matters of religion, this fact in no sense meant separation of church and state. Royal decrees in 1815 and 1835 provided that the administration of all church affairs in Indonesia be separated from the church in Holland and turned over to the Ministry of Colonies. Thus the Governor General, acting through a church board in Djakarta, exercised absolute control over the Church of the Indies in all matters, from the appointment of clergy and oversight of finances to the approval of session members and trustees elected by local congregations. It is not difficult to concur with the comment of a competent observer that this amounted to "state administration of spiritual goods," with the clergy being the state-appointed and salaried administrators. The 1835 decree provided for 43 ministers and 31 assistant ministers (all Europeans), 9 religious teachers and 350 Indonesian gospel teachers, a ministry considerably larger than any that existed under the Dutch East India Company. Nevertheless considerable dissatisfaction arose—interestingly, more from the side of the state than from that of the church. Several commissions were appointed to study the question and formulate proposals for change, in 1863-1874, 1899-1900 and 1915, but the administrative separation of the Protestant church from the colonial government came only in the 1930's. Financial separation was effected in 1950, only after Independence.

King William's ideal of a unified Protestant church in the Indies was short lived. New theological controversies in Holland in the nineteenth century led to the establishment in 1873 in Djakarta of the first congregation of the Gereformeerd Church in Holland. But far more significant was the gradual growth of churches in various regions of Indonesia as a result of the work of the foreign missionary societies that flourished in the West from the beginning of the nineteenth

century. By the end of the century the Church of the Indies, with its
four branches in the Moluccas, Minahasa, Timor and Western Indonesia, was no longer the only Protestant church in the archipelago.

In the century from 1830 to 1930 the efforts of Dutch, German,
Swiss and American missionaries in Indonesia planted and nourished
more than 30 regional churches, which in 1964 had a membership of
two and a quarter million, or more than one and one-half times the
membership of the Protestant church in Indonesia. The growth in
diversity has even greater significance for the church in Indonesia
than the growth in numbers. The emergence of these 30 churches has
meant that Protestant Christianity has become national in scope rather
than being found primarily among the minority peoples of East Indonesia, as was true of the Church of the Indies. But this development
has also meant that the problem of the unity of the church has become
a dominant concern of Indonesian Protestant leadership today.

The table at the front of the book shows that beginning with the
1930's the Protestant churches now in the Council of Churches
achieved autonomy both from government and from church bodies
outside Indonesia. The administrative separation of church from state
reduced government control over the churches but did not end it completely because the financial separation did not come until 1950. More
important than the formal establishment of autonomous churches,
however, was the fact that under the Japanese occupation (1942-1945)
and the revolutionary struggle for Independence (1945-1949), prac-
tically all foreign personnel were removed from the Indonesian
churches so that they became self-supporting, self-governing and self-
propagating for the first time. This giant step, despite the severe hardship it entailed, was most salutary in movement toward the independent selfhood of the Indonesian churches.

The fact that Indonesian Christians joined their fellow citizens of
other faiths in the nationalist struggle against colonial subjection did
much to remove the stigma of "foreignness" or "Dutchness" that had
adhered to Christianity. One result was that the Christian religion
became one of the "recognized" religions in the newly established
Republic of Indonesia based on the Five Principles. Another result
was that after Independence the Indonesian churches, completely freed
from the limitations of colonialism, began to grow both in numbers
and in the depth and spread of their influence on Indonesian life.
In both of these respects it has been observed by recent visitors that
the Indonesian churches presently constitute perhaps the most vigorous and fastest growing church in the world.

The Roman Catholic Church

Roman Catholicism is the oldest form of Christianity in Indonesia. Roman Catholic missionary activity began in the Moluccas (the Spice Islands in East Indonesia) during the 1530's under Portuguese protection. Francis Xavier spent much of 1546 there helping lay solid foundations for a promising beginning made by the Franciscans, Jesuits, Dominicans and other orders. Sharp opposition from Islamic forces in Atjeh and the Moluccas produced the first Christian martyrs in Indonesia before 1600. Even so, by the end of the sixteenth century Catholic Christians numbered around 50,000.

With the ousting of the Portuguese by the Dutch in 1605, the Netherlands East India Company enforced the principle then practiced throughout Europe: *cuius regio eius religio,* meaning that believers were expected to embrace the faith of the civil authority. Applied to Indonesia this meant Reformed Christianity. Partly for political but also for religious reasons, the Company prevented the spread of Catholicism during its period of rule; nevertheless, Catholicism did not completely disappear.

During the third period of Catholic history in Indonesia, 1800–1945, the colonial government permitted Catholic missionaries to work in certain areas where they had already labored, notably on Java, Flores, North Sulawesi and Borneo. For a time there was conflict between government and church over the appointment and status of priests, whom the government wished to control as it did the clergy in the Protestant state church. But by 1847 efforts by the Roman Catholics to separate church administration from the state were successful, and Catholic missions advanced as a result. The first apostolic prefecture was established in 1826 and was followed in 1845 by the appointment of a vicar apostolic. Educational work was given special emphasis by the Society of Jesus, the dominant order in Indonesia, which invited other orders to assist them.

The period since Independence has seen remarkable growth in the Roman Catholic Church, due in part to the full extension of religious liberty to all. This has meant freedom to work anywhere in Indonesia; and the government extended various kinds of aid to educational, charitable and even religious work of the Roman church as well as to other recognized religious groups. Theological education and the training of a native clergy received special emphasis, because in 1939 there were only 15 Indonesians in the total of 544 priests in the country. A similar condition prevailed in the lay orders.

In 1964 the Roman Catholic Church in Indonesia was divided into six metropolitan sees with 19 suffragans, two vicariates apostolic and three prefectures apostolic. Centers of Catholic work, with archdiocesan cathedrals, were in Djakarta, Ende (Flores), Makassar (South Sulawesi), Pontianak (Kalimantan), Medan (North Sumatra) and Semarang (Central Java). The following church statistics are given in *The New Catholic Encyclopedia.*

> Catholics totaled about 1.5 million concentrated on the island of Flores. This was a great increase over their 275,000 in 1923, of whom 64,000 were Europeans. There were 30 bishops (4 native), 1,356 priests (220 native), 700 brothers (272 native) and 3,270 sisters (1,360 native). Catholics maintained 3 universities, with more than 7,000 students. . . . Catholics operated also 2,414 elementary schools with 403,760 students; 520 secondary schools with 101,075 students; 49 normal schools with 4,950 students; 134 professional schools, with 10,200 students; 77 hospitals; and 68 orphanages. There were 20 minor seminaries, with 1,780 students, and 3 major seminaries for secular clergy and 8 for religious, with a total of 360 students.[1]

Like the Protestant churches, the Roman Catholic Church in Indonesia has played a significant role in national affairs. There is a vigorous Catholic political party (*Partai Katolik*) and a number of Catholic mass organizations that mobilize youth, university students, women, laborers, artists and farmers for social action. Catholics are well represented in both legislative and executive branches of government. Catholic publications include a daily paper in Djakarta, three weekly magazines and six monthlies.

The following quotation will reveal something of the broad conception that underlies contemporary Catholic mission in Indonesia.

> At present what is required is this: not to ignore the existing social structure, but to study, to utilize, and develop it for the better; not to isolate the pupils from their social and cultural environment in a kind of education which is too subservient to Western programmes, but to develop the students in their social context as an irradiating ferment; not just to present charity to the poor, the sick, the destitute, and the orphans, but—as the genuine conception of social apostolate has it—to better the structures of this world and to integrate whatever is sound in the social patterns into a dynamic Christian community. Proselytising in which single individuals are disrupted from their socio-religious

milieu presents the missions with the nearly insoluble problem of re-integration: how to create a vital community out of an amorphous group of alienated individuals. But once engaged in a communal approach towards the existential social forces in the people, the mission will, by sheer force of self-propelling growth, commit itself more and more to participation in nation-building.

The Catholic Church in Indonesia has no other choice than that of overall social and national commitment—not because of opportunism, but out of inner conviction, confronted with the *kairos* of the present situation. The message of the last great encyclicals and that of Vatican II make clear that such a kind of social apostolate is the answer to the signs of the time, and fits in organically with the whole doctrine of the Church. In the poverty-stricken and disintegrated society of Indonesia, the Church needs to be conscious of her responsibility for the improvement of the social structure and for economic development, in which her supernatural vocation will be transparent.[2]

This picture reveals that the Roman Catholic Church is a vigorous, widely dispersed, solidly rooted, actively engaged segment of the total Christian community in Indonesia. In recent years, especially since the Second Vatican Council, contacts and cooperation between the Catholic and Protestant branches of Christ's church have multiplied greatly and show bright promise for ecumenical efforts in the years ahead.

Protestant Bodies Outside the Council

Protestant Christians outside the Indonesia Council of Churches comprise one grouping only for purposes of analysis. Actually six categories can be distinguished.

First, there are several churches whose applications for membership in the Council are pending, some for as long as 10 years. Some of these have grown out of schism, for example, the Indonesian Christian Church (*Huria Kristen Indonesia*) and the Indonesian Christian Protestant Church (*Geredja Kristen Protestan Indonesia*), both of which split off from the Batak Christian Protestant Church (*Huria Kristen Batak Protestan*), in 1945 and 1963 respectively. In these cases, nontheological factors were largely responsible for the schism. The *Parepatan Agung*, or Christian Church of North Central Java, does not have a schismatic origin but experienced an abortive union with the Central Java Christian Church in 1949, from which it separated again in 1953. The Council of Churches has been unwilling to accept these and similar churches into membership until every means has been exhausted of reconciling them with the council member churches from which they are estranged.

A second group consists of Christian bodies that cooperate with the Indonesia Council of Churches but are not members because they do not consider themselves churches. The largest of these, the Salvation Army, whose home base is in Great Britain, began work in Indonesia in 1894. Its officers originate from various countries as well as various regions in Indonesia. Evangelistic work is carried on in Sulawesi, the Moluccas, Timor, Java, Kalimantan and North and South Sumatra. A variety of services to society, including schools, hospitals and clinics, orphanages, hostels for students and homes for the aged as well as relief programs for the destitute are operating in Sulawesi, Sumatra and especially Java. The headquarters of the Salvation Army is in Bandung. The 1953 listing of the Department of Religion mentioned 61 officers and 35,000 members, and the number is much larger now.

The Overseas Missionary Fellowship, a metamorphosis of the China Inland Mission, has been working in Indonesia since the early 1950's. Like Salvation Army workers, OMF workers come from many lands and as many church backgrounds but are united in their conservative evangelical faith. The OMF works by contributing personnel on invitation of local bodies—congregations or educational, medical and other institutions. Most of its 45 or 50 missionaries are concentrated on Java, but 14 are on Sumatra, Sulawesi and Borneo.

A third grouping includes other schismatic groups that have split off from the major regional churches in North Sumatra, Nias and Minahasa. They have no relations with missionary societies outside Indonesia and have made no effort to join the Council. Nontheological factors, such as church discipline or personal differences, accounted for the original division.

The fourth category includes churches and mission bodies, similar to those in the Council, which for particular reasons do not choose to cooperate. Most of these have developed from foreign missionary activity begun since World War I and have entered the so-called "untouched fields." Oldest and best established is the Christian and Missionary Alliance (CMA), an American based church that began work in 1929 from headquarters in Makassar. By 1938 they counted 81 congregations served by 26 missionaries, ministering to a baptized membership of 10,731 in Sulawesi, Buton and Moeni, Bali, Lombok, Sumbawa, South Sumatra, Banka and Billiton, Kalimantan and Irian

Barat. Since World War II the work has expanded considerably, to include Bandung and Djakarta on Java and Roti, Flores and Alor in East Indonesia. The headquarters office is now in Djakarta and there are 58 CMA missionaries at work in Indonesia. The most recent figures (1964) indicate a far-flung enterprise: 68,000 members in 452 organized congregations and 150 unorganized groups, more than 500 being self-supporting; more than 500 national workers and employees, of whom at least 75 are ordained. Baptisms in 1964 were over the 3,000 mark, with nearly 6,500 enquirers. The literature program produced more than 11 million pages. An important advance was achieved in 1965 with the formation of one national organization (*Kemah Indjil Geredja Masehi Indonesia*) with six districts: East Kalimantan, West Kalimantan, East Indonesia, Java, Irian Barat and the Lesser Sunda Islands. The major institutions that serve all the districts—the publication ministry and Jaffray School of Theology—were placed under the authority of this national body. Three Bible schools graduated 30 evangelists and had a combined enrollment of 136 in 1966. The CMA has established a widely spread national movement, which appears to have solid roots in both national leadership and financial support.

The World Evangelization Crusade, with headquarters in Kalimantan, works on Java, Sumatra and West Kalimantan, largely among those as yet unreached by the gospel. This is also the case with the Go Ye Followship in the same areas, and of the Conservative Baptists and the Regions Beyond Mission. There is close cooperation between these bodies and the CMA.

A fifth group is made up of bodies often referred to by Indonesian church leaders as *bidaat* (sects), because they are late-comers that live around the edges of the Indonesian churches and often appear to grow at their expense. Church leaders frequently cite, as the most recent example, the Southern Baptist Church from the USA, which entered Indonesia on Christmas Day, 1951. The Southern Baptists have developed work largely on Java and in the large cities, Bandung, Djakarta, Palembang, Semarang, Jogjakarta, Surabaja and Kediri. In addition to local congregations in these places, usually led by a missionary, a publications program is located in Bandung (West Java), a large hospital has been operating in Kediri (East Java) since 1957, a clinic in Bukittinggi (1963) and a theological school in Semarang (Central Java) since 1954. In 1957 there were 31 missionaries at work in Indonesia, and by 1967 the number had grown to 84. The Southern Baptists have eschewed the more remote fields in favor of areas where other churches have long been at work. (The first Baptist "home missionary" was sent out by the congregations in East Java, in 1965, to a predominantly Christian area in the Moluccas!) In several places where they have worked, dissatisfaction has arisen on the part of existing churches as they have seen their young people attracted to American style programs in well-equipped facilities. Perhaps this resentment would pass in time if the Southern Baptists would enter into cooperation with the Indonesian churches, but this is contrary to the mission's firm policy. The annual report for 1967 gives a membership of 3,965 in 19 congregations, and 42 national pastors help serve these and 51 other mission points.

The Seventh Day Adventists' work in Indonesia is presently divided into East and West Indonesia Union Missions. The first, with headquarters in Manado, includes Sulawesi, Sangir-Talaud and Ambon. The headquarters of the second is Djakarta, supervising eight local missions in Java, Sumatra, Kalimantan and Southeast Indonesia. A considerable printing enterprise that produces literature for all Indonesia operates from Bandung. Medical work, also based in Bandung and operating through clinics in several regions, is one of the ministries emphasized by the Adventists with support from their home base in America. In 1967 they reported 40 missionaries in the field and 36,000 adult baptized members.

Also in this fifth category are many of the Pentecostal bodies that entered Indonesia between the two world wars.

In general the Christian groups included in this fifth category emphasize personal evangelism, using revivalist methods current in the United States. In some, spiritual healing is stressed. In matters of faith, if not always in practice, they are conservative orthodox. Some regional councils of churches report participation by local congregations of these groups in ecumenical observance of Christian holy days.

The last type of organization to be mentioned has a debatable relationship to Christianity. It consists of groups in Batakland ("*Bijbelkring*") and Nias ("*Fa'awosa*") that reflect syncretism between Christian and indigenous religious elements. Also included would be the Jehovah's Witnesses and Christian Science groups that came to Indonesia quite recently from America.

What Kind of Protestant Christianity?

How shall we describe the Protestant churches in Indonesia? Here we view them briefly from the perspectives of their theological and ecclesiastical backgrounds and certain nontheological, nonecclesiastical factors, trusting that a general picture will emerge.

At least five of the churches originated within or close to the Church of the Indies and its predecessor, the Dutch East India Company church. The others, in contrast, originated from missionary activity. Because the latter did not grow up in the bureaucratic, traditional spirit of the old state church, they appear more vigorous, missionary minded and flexible.

In regard to ecclesiastical tradition, the majority, at least 25, are predominantly Calvinist. Two have Methodist background; two are Mennonite; at least three come from the Pentecostal tradition; and three, coming out of the German national church tradition, are related to the Lutheran World Federation. In terms of membership then, perhaps a million Indonesian Protestants, or one in four, come from other than the Calvinist branch of the Reformation.

Another way to look at the ecclesiastical background would be to note that while the great majority, perhaps 25 churches, were related to Dutch churches or missionary societies; at least four have relationships with German churches; three grew out of American missionary efforts; and one came from Swiss labors. Several seem not to have been related to any overseas church.

To picture the theological complexion of Indonesian churches is difficult. There are no "liberal" or "modernist" churches or groups, in the American sense, though it is not difficult to find those with no clear-cut, consistent theological position, particularly in churches formerly included in the Church of the Indies, which was not a confessional church. Most of the churches are theologically orthodox or conservative. The Heidelberg Confession is widely used where a theological norm is needed. Most are strongly traditional, whatever the particular tradition may be, and fairly inflexible in outlook. Those in the Pentecostal, Methodist and Mennonite families tend, perhaps, to be more flexible, less traditional in spirit. A generalization that held, until recently, would be that theology is for the church, confined within the church; it is not for the world, to be related to problems of everyday life in the world.

There are also important nontheological, nonecclesiastical factors at work. These appear to be more important in the problem of Christian unity, certainly in church union explorations, than the ecclesiastical or theological factors. Some of the churches came directly out of primal religious beliefs, that is to say, were formed by people who laid aside their autochthonous religion and entered the Christian faith by groups, often whole villages at a time. This is true of 19 churches, found mostly in East Indonesia and Sumatra. These are the largest and in some cases the oldest churches. In contrast, there are at least 15 churches whose members have come, one by one as it were, from other Asian religions such as Buddhism, Hinduism or Islam. This is true of most of the churches found in the central part of Indonesia, particularly on Java. In numbers they are relatively small, only a tiny minority in their regions.

A part of this same phenomenon is the fact that 12 of the churches might be called "ethnic churches," while 22 others can be termed "gathered churches." "Ethnic church," in this context, means the Christian community in an area where a majority of the people have accepted the faith and come into the church. Thus a member of that ethnic group is usually identified as a Christian. There has been a "marriage" between the indigenous culture and the Christian faith in such areas, for example, in Minahasa and Batak-land. "Gathered churches" refers to situations where the Christian community comprises a small group gathered from the majority people adhering to the "great tradition," which the Christian faith and church have not yet penetrated. Churches on Java and Bali are examples.

One more perspective from which to view the Indonesian churches would be to observe that about one-third of the churches serve people living in towns or cities, while approximately two-thirds are found in rural areas. (We are speaking here of member churches in the Council, not of local congregations. If the latter were included, a still higher percentage would be rural.) The Protestant churches thus reflect fairly accurately the present urban-rural balance in Indonesia.

FOOTNOTES
1. *The New Catholic Encyclopedia*, 1967. New York: McGraw-Hill, pp. 480-481.
2. Herder correspondence, February, 1966, pp. 60-61.

4 The Churches of East and Southeast Indonesia

The Church in East Indonesia

EAST INDONESIA IS ONE OF TWO REGIONS where Christianity developed earliest and most widely.

1 **The Indonesia Protestant Church (Geredja Protestan Indonesia)** is the largest unit in the Indonesia Council of Churches—but it has no members! They are to be found in the four churches who together constitute the General Synod of the Protestant Church. The four are: the Protestant Church of the Moluccas, the Evangelical Christian Church of Timor, the Evangelical Christian Church of Minahasa, and the Western Indonesia Protestant Church. These autonomous churches are members of the Council and have their own synods. They join for certain purposes in the Protestant Church, which constitutes the largest, the oldest and the most widespread church body in Indonesia, recording in 1967 nearly 1,500,000 members, 1,850 congregations and 575 fully ordained ministers.

The history of this church is inseparable from the history of Dutch colonial rule in Indonesia.[1] It was built on the Roman Catholic foundation laid during the Portuguese period (1520–1605). It was administered by the Netherlands East India Company from 1605 to 1800, being part of and contributing to the Company's operations in Indonesia. But it grew very little during those two centuries, except in traditional structures, attitudes and practices that were to hang like millstones around its neck in later times. As soon as the Dutch colonial administration was restored after the Napoleonic wars in Europe, the brief burst of new life and missionary activity that appeared between 1820 and 1850 was brought completely under the control of the state and remained so until the decade before World War II. It was administered from Batavia, the colonial capital, by a Church Board (*Kerkbestuur*) consisting of a member of the Council of the Indies (the government), who served as chairman, the Protestant ministers in Djakarta, one of whom was vice-chairman, and three prominent members of the Djakarta congregation. But in reality this board had only advisory powers; the Governor General of the Indies made all decisions about personnel changes, disciplinary matters, finances, and so on.

In 1934 the Minahasan Church was granted administrative autonomy by the Dutch Crown. A year later the Moluccan Church followed. It was not until 1947 and 1948 respectively that the Timor Church and the Western Indonesia Church were separated from the administration of the colonial government. Interestingly, these churches have all grown substantially since achieving autonomy and transferring to indigenous leadership, the last two mentioned more than doubling their membership.

2   **The Moluccan Protestant Church (Geredja Protestan Maluku)** is the oldest evangelical church in Asia.[2] It serves a fragmented island province in Eastern Indonesia long noted for the production of cloves and nutmeg. The more than 1,000 coral islands, with a land area of 74,505 square kilometers, support an almost wholly agricultural population of more than 900,000. Slightly under half are Christian; about 47 percent embrace Islam; the remainder are animists and members of other minuscule religious minorities. During the Portuguese and Company periods there was sharp competition between Islam and Christianity for the religious loyalty of the people. By the middle of the nineteenth century, the present rough balance between Muslim and Christian communities was already established, although the size of the remaining religious minorities was larger then. Since Independence (1950 for the Moluccas), the religious problem has become more vital, and tension between Muslims and Christians has increased,

largely because Muslims now constitute the majority in Indonesia.
At the same time, the indigenous cultural and even religious traditions
tend to provide some common basis of unity for the two groups.
Because they are traditional in outlook and spirit, however, both religious communities have been strongly challenged by the rapid pace
of social, economic, political and cultural change, which has accelerated at an increasing pace since 1950.

Stimulated both by these external pressures and by internal developments, especially the new clergy produced by the theological schools
since 1950, the Protestant Church of the Moluccas has entered a period
of momentous reform and renewal.[3] One is reminded of the new life
and evangelical vigor with which Moluccan Christians responded to
the work of Joseph Kam and other European missionaries in the
decades following 1817, which produced an indigenous missionary
spirit and tradition that has been important in providing Ambonese
preachers and teachers for outreach throughout East Indonesia.

For the past decade the Moluccan Church has struggled mightily
with itself and within the revolutionary milieu of Moluccan society to
renew its life and ministry and to reform its structures for stronger
and more effective witness and service. This struggle began in 1956
with the decision of the 18th Synod to establish a department of
evangelism. The 19th Synod felt it was necessary to attempt to recon-
struct the life of the local congregation before the church could become
missionary minded. The 20th issued a message summoning the whole
church to repentance, renewal and surrender to the Word of God.
Finally, the 22nd Synod, meeting in 1964, took an historic action
directing the executive committee "to take all necessary steps to change
the situation of mere verbal confession concerning Jesus Christ, His
Church and His World, to a self-conscious confession whose meaning
and full implications are understood and accepted." This meant, almost immediately, a radical restructuring of theological education and
leadership training, as well as of the pattern of administration and
leadership of the Synod office. It has also meant a full liberation of the
potential for witness and service of laymen in a church that for
centuries had been dominated by clergy. This in turn makes possible
a development of stewardship that could eventually provide resources
needed by the church to perform an expanded ministry to the
Moluccan region and to all Indonesia.

Thus this little-known, oldest evangelical church in Asia with
380,000 members, 673 congregations and 403 ordained ministers is
among the more active, creative, self-reforming churches in Asia today.

3   **The Timor Evangelical Christian Church (Geredja Masehi Indjili Timor)** shares the general outlines of the history of the Protestant Church of the Netherlands Indies (*Indisch Kerk*).

The first Dutch pastor came for a time in 1612, but there was no regular ministry to build on the Roman Catholic beginnings until 1670–1688, and again in 1753–1758. Probably because the Netherlands East India Company had no major commercial interests, like the Moluccan spice trade in Southeast Indonesia, it was not until 1821 that there was a continuous ministry in Timor. This ministry also served the surrounding region, including the islands of Roti and Sawu, and was responsible for perhaps 20,000 souls.

As with the Moluccas, the development of the church under the Dutch colonial government underwent two distinct periods of contrasting influence. The first was that of the Netherlands Missionary Society, whose missionaries and policies dominated from 1821 to 1863. The second was the period of *Indisch Kerk* administration, from 1863 to 1942. But even so, because of difficult health conditions for Westerners and poor communications, continuous ministry and supervision was spotty. Not until the 1930's did large numbers of people begin to come into the church from the interior regions of Timor and Alor. Then mass Christianization occurred so rapidly that the church did not have sufficient personnel to instruct all the new members. This fact led to unfortunate situations of syncretism or nominal Christianity in places. The Timor Church has a background of indigenous religion and culture. The fact that the Timor Church became autonomous only in 1947, after the Japanese occupation, suggests that it was somewhat less advanced than the other branches of the Indonesia Protestant Church. But since then it has been one of the fastest growing churches in Indonesia. With a membership of 223,881 in 315 congregations in 1948 and 300,000 members served by 80 pastors in 1958, today it has a membership of 650,000 and a territory embracing all of East Nusa Tenggara province, which has a population of nearly two million.

The conditions under which this church has grown and now must carry on its work provide the background for its main problems. Recall that the church in Timor was controlled by and has been described as a tool of the colonial government and that until recently it was in a geographically isolated region with little economic and cultural development. Thus there is a great scarcity of trained leadership to carry on an increasingly heavy task in the church itself and in Timorese society. There is also a limited economic base to provide the resources required by a rapidly growing church. Schools and churches, to mention only the traditional forms of ministry, do not have the resources needed for qualitative and quantitative growth and wider ministries. It is an old church and a large church, a member of the Indonesia Council of Churches and of the World Council of Churches. But it is not yet a strong church. Historically it has had relations with the Dutch Reformed Church, and since the early 1950's with the American Mennonites and the Australian Methodists and Presbyterians. But the Evangelical Christian Church of Timor needs and hopes for more help from sister churches in Indonesia and overseas.

4   **The Minahasa Evangelical Christian Church (Geredja Masehi Indjili Minahasa)** is one of the largest and potentially strongest churches in Indonesia.

Minahasa lies on the northern tip of Sulawesi and comprises an area (3,050 square miles) about two and one-half times the size of Rhode Island. Of the population of nearly 700,000, about 600,000 are Christians. The region is one of the more highly developed in Indonesia, hence communications within the area do not present the problem they do in Timor and the Moluccas.

During the period of Portuguese and Spanish ascendancy (1560-1663), a small group of Roman Catholic Christians formed. No serious attention was paid to Minahasa until after 1822 when, at the urging of Joseph Kam, the Netherlands Missionary Society began work with some 3,000 baptized but largely uninstructed members of five congregations. By 1870, as a result of well-conceived evangelistic efforts by the Netherlands Missionary Society, the basic task of Christianizing Minahasa was completed. As in Timor and the Moluccas, the people came to Christianity in Minahasa out of tribal religion.

In contrast to the speed and ease of evangelization, the development of church organization in Minahasa was unusually backward. As late as 1890 there was no synod or presbytery.

When in 1876 the colonial government transferred Christian work in Minahasa from the Missionary Society to the state church, the membership was already 80,000. Only after the organizational system of the Protestant church was introduced did there develop any sense of being a church, even though the church administration was part of civil government both in spirit and in financing. The chief minister was located in Manado, the capital city. Beneath him in 1934 were 11 "as-

sistant ministers," mostly Europeans; "teachers of the gospel," Minahasans who had received instruction in a training school established in
1886; and 27 "teachers of the congregation" (*Guru Djumat*), school
teachers who had received a little specialized training to conduct worship. There was no prescribed confession of faith or catechism. Each
local leader did as he thought best, under the supervision of his
superior.

Thus when it became autonomous in 1934 the Minahasan Church
was an ethnic church with a collective mentality but almost no experience in self-government, at least on the part of laymen in local
congregations and regional groupings. A church order and organization, with sessions at the local level and 11 presbyteries that chose
delegates to the Synod of the Minahasan Church, was submitted for
approval by the first Synod.

The Japanese occupation and the revolution radically changed the
situation. The Reverend A. Z. R. Wenas, a Minahasan minister, became Moderator of the Synod in 1942 and gave fearless leadership
during the difficult days of the Japanese occupation. Developments by
the end of the decade led to the complete independence of the
Minahasan Church from the government, especially when all government subsidies to the church were suddenly and permanently ended
early in 1950.

Since then the church in Minahasa has faced many challenges from
within and without. Secularism has grown steadily stronger because of
the desire for progress, especially in economic life and in education.
The formal and traditional character of Minahasan Christianity as it
developed within the state church is fair game for secularizing influences. It is also fair game for competition from other Christian
groups. Together the Roman Catholics and 23 Protestant "sects" (so
viewed by the Minahasan Church) have won more than 100,000 ad-
herents in Minahasa. The 1958-1961 PERMESTA rebellion of Minahasans against the central government brought much strife, destruction
and suffering, both physical and spiritual, to the region. Through this
tense and trying time, the church leadership sought with considerable
success to reconcile the conflicting parties.

A total of 500,000 members are found in 502 congregations, served
by 110 ordained ministers and 500 assistant ministers. It operates more
than 400 primary and 35 secondary schools and one university with
both theological and general education faculties. Two general and
six maternity hospitals, 28 clinics and five orphanages constitute its
social and health ministry. The American churches, in particular the

Disciples of Christ, the Church of the Brethren, and the Evangelical Covenant Church and the Netherlands Missionary Society cooperate with the Minahasan Church, especially to develop urgently needed new leadership.

5 The Western Indonesia Protestant Church (Geredja Protestan Indonesia Bagian Barat) is "the fourth church." It was made up of congregations composed of Dutchmen, Indo-Europeans, Ambonese, Timorese and Minahasans working in posts in Dutch firms, in the military or in the civil service in the cities in Western Indonesia. The Protestant Church of Indonesia, it will be recalled, was administered through Djakarta, with headquarters at Immanuel Church, across from the main railway station.

The Western Indonesia Church was the last of the four branches of the state church to be granted autonomy from the colonial government. This occurred in 1948 at the end of Dutch colonial rule in Indonesia, while the war for Independence was being fought. Until 1957 there were separate Dutch and Indonesian language congregations. The two often used the same church building until 1958, when the Western Indonesia Church dispensed with Dutch language in the heat of the struggle with Holland over the control of Irian Barat.

Unlike the other three churches, the Western Indonesia Church is not an ethnic church. Its members come from at least three diverse ethnic groups, and thus it feels ethnic as well as urban tensions. Its members are not native to the region in which they live, having migrated from East Indonesia to the cities in West Indonesia. Thus, more than the other churches, it has until recently existed primarily to provide worship and pastoral care for its own members, rather than to undertake a mission of witness and service to the people of the region.

The ministers of the Western Indonesia Church are, like the members, persons originating from one of the other three churches, though in recent years it has begun to produce its own ministry. Another reason for the weaker leadership situation in the Western Indonesia Church is that the influence of the Dutch remained dominant at least a decade longer than it did in the other three churches.

Today the Western Indonesia Protestant Church numbers approximately 350,000 members, found in 89 congregations served by 57 ordained ministers. The number of congregations has nearly doubled in the last 15 years, while the total number of ministers has increased only 14 percent. At the same time an increasing percentage of ministers

(35 percent in 1966) are serving in capacities other than local congregations, for example, military chaplaincy.

Within the last few years, perhaps because of political factors, a considerable effort has been made, especially on the initiative of the Western Indonesia Church, to bring these four churches into greater unity and to recover the reality of the one Protestant Church of Indonesia, which existed in colonial days. It is still too early to evaluate this development, the motivations behind it, and the possible effects on other Indonesian churches if it were to succeed. But it is a significant factor in the ecumenical scene today, if only because these four churches together constitute the oldest, the largest and the most far-flung church body in Indonesia, as well as perhaps the one most deeply marked by the Dutch colonial legacy.

Two other churches in East Indonesia have historical connections with either the Company church or the *Indisch Kerk*.

6 **The Halmahera Evangelical Christian Church (Geredja Masehi Indjili Halmahera)** became autonomous in 1949. Today it has a membership of around 50,000, with 240 congregations served by only 20 ministers.

During the Portuguese period, Francis Xavier (in 1546) and other Roman Catholic missionaries made converts and established a church in Halmahera where, led by the Sultans of Ternate and Tidore, Islam was the dominant religion. But when first the Portuguese and later the Dutch made Ambon their headquarters in the Moluccas, Islamic power prevailed. As a result, the church in Halmahera was decimated, in a struggle that produced the first Indonesian martyrs to the faith.

The East India Company had no commercial objects in Halmahera, so the region received little attention. Consequently the church disappeared and Islam dominated the region for the next two centuries.

In 1866 the Utrecht Missionary Society sent missionaries to make a fresh start in Halmahera. Active opposition on the part of Islam, indifference on the part of the colonial authorities (resulting from the policy of religious neutralism) and poor economic conditions in the region combined to make progress extremely difficult. The first substantial fruits began to appear at the end of the century, and during the first two decades of the twentieth century rapid advances were made in Christianizing people of animistic background in the region.

There were too few indigenous workers to assist the handful of missionaries sent by the Utrecht Missionary Society. Ambonese teachers were introduced to give leadership to schools and local congregations, but they were not well prepared and did not understand the language or culture of the people. Consequently careful instruction in the faith was lacking, and Christianity did not penetrate too deeply into the life of the people. The number of baptized persons increased, but the number of confirmed Christians eligible to receive the sacrament and be elected deacon or elder remained infinitesimal. Other efforts such as schools and coconut plantations operated by the church also experienced slow growth because of difficult conditions. Geographic isolation, weak leadership and economic underdevelopment all conspired to hinder the growth of the Halmahera Church.

After it became autonomous, the Halmahera Church entered into ecumenical cooperation with the Mennonite Central Committee in the United States with the aim of making the plantations more productive and giving medical and health service. Still progress has been slow and spotty. The organization of a regional council of churches in the Moluccas early in 1967 may help strengthen the Halmahera Church.

7 **The Sangir-Talaud Evangelical Christian Church (Geredja Masehi Indjili Sangir-Talaud)** also goes back to the period of the Portuguese and Spanish ascendancy. The islands lie northeast of the Minahasa region in the direction of Mindanao in the Philippines, once a Spanish colony. The Christianization of the people by Roman Catholic efforts was well along by the time the Dutch displaced the Spanish in 1677. These islands fell within the jurisdiction of the Dutch ministers assigned to Manado and Ternate, but actually, during the East India Company period (up to 1800), little pastoral care was available to this sizable Christian community in Sangir-Talaud. Some Ambonese teachers were sent to help with the schools and congregations, but pastoral care was inadequate. From a report on a pastoral visit in 1854, we learn that there were estimated to be 20,000 Christians and 24 churches, served largely by Ambonese teacher-preachers paid by the colonial government. None of these baptized Christians were confirmed and, according to the practice of the Company church, could therefore not receive the Lord's Supper; nor were there any ministers available to administer the sacraments. Only about 3 percent of the Christians had had schooling. Consequently the church was at a decidedly low ebb when the missionaries entered in 1855.

Dutch artisan-missionaries worked under great difficulties with varying degrees of success until the end of the century. After better support was provided by the government, steady progress was made between 1903 and 1940, not only in the congregations but also in school and social work. But because leadership, especially the number of ministers, was inadequate to serve the region, the quality of Christian faith and life left much to be desired. Under the colonial situation, with financial resources supplied by the government, funds were never sufficient for programs of ministerial training.

The Sangir-Talaud Church became autonomous in 1947, after preparations that had begun in 1934. But the question of a church organization to fit the conditions has proved difficult to solve. The congregations are spread across several islands, without efficient means of communication. How can the Synod best administer and serve the church? Also, because of dense population and economic limitations, large numbers of people have emigrated to Java, Sulawesi and the Philippines. How are they to be related to and ministered to by the Sangir-Talaud Church? Congregations of Sangir-Talaud emigrés have developed on Java and on Mindanao. Is this wise or necessary?

At present the Sangir-Talaud Church has approximately 200,000 members in 275 congregations served by 108 ministers. It operates numerous schools and other service institutions. In 1966 a major volcanic eruption caused much destruction. Outside churches provided resources to help meet this need through interchurch aid.

8   **The West Irian Evangelical Christian Church (Geredja Kristen Indjili di Irian Barat).** In 1963, the Republic of Indonesia gained sovereignty over Irian Barat (West Irian). Irian Barat is part of the world's largest island and one of the most sparsely populated regions in the world (1.8 persons per square kilometer). The total population is perhaps four million, of whom three quarters of a million live in the western section. Only at the beginning of the twentieth century did this section become actively administered by the colonial government. Because of the rugged topography and the inhospitable climate, the population consists of many small, isolated tribes that have developed distinct languages and cultures. Islam had been introduced in the northwestern coastal areas by Muslim traders from North Moluccas. Christianity has spread with increasing tempo, beginning in the coastal settlements, since the end of the last century. Of the 860,000 people, 170,000 are now Protestants and more than 40,000 are Roman Catholics, while at least 15,000 embrace Islam.

Before 1860 several efforts had been made to plant the gospel on Irian soil, but the difficult living conditions forced withdrawal. Of the 18 missionaries sent by the Utrecht Missionary Society up to 1900, only three continued working in the area, so great were the difficulties. For the first 25 years after the Utrecht Missionary Society sent its first workers into West Irian in 1862, progress was almost nil; only 20 persons had received baptism by 1887. After 50 years of continuous missionary activities, however, results began to appear. In the first decades of the twentieth century, as the colonial government began to develop the region, requests came for educational and evangelistic work in various districts, and by 1920 all the coastal regions and islands had been reached. In 1931 there were 25,000 baptized Christians. By 1940 this number had jumped to 80,000, and today there are 170,000 members of Protestant bodies on Irian Barat.

World War II left a profound impact on Irian Barat. After the war new missionary organizations, largely from the United States,* began to penetrate the high plateaus and deep valleys of the interior. There, scattered in widely separated areas, were small tribes of people, some of whom were still living at the Stone Age level of cultural development. The gospel and the efforts of the missionaries in literacy, education, health and other fields have helped to pacify and develop these peoples, preparing them for life in the twentieth century.

In recent years serious efforts have been undertaken to gather all Protestant Christians in Irian Barat into a unified church. A large step in this direction was made in 1956, with the establishment of the West Irian Evangelical Christian Church. Other groups, such as the two Presbyteries of the Protestant Church in the Moluccas in Fak Fak and Merauke, have indicated a willingness to move toward a unified church, but there is still a long way to go.

The transfer of sovereignty from Holland to Indonesia in 1963, while solving a difficult political conflict, has meant a transition that has brought to Irian Barat all the problems inherent in the Indonesian revolutionary experience. Now that it is under the Indonesian administration, stronger pressures from Islam are being felt. Tensions heightened around the Malaysia confrontation and the turbulence following the October, 1965 coup attempt. The attempt to integrate Irian Barat into the badly shattered economy of Indonesia has also brought problems.

---

* The main ones being Unevangelized Fields Mission, the Regions Beyond Missionary Union, the Evangelical Alliance Mission and the Christian and Missionary Alliance.

On the brighter side, the achievement of independence may be expected to provide new stimulus for evangelization and church growth in West Irian as it has in almost every other region of Indonesia. The West Irian Church has requested and received, from member churches of the Council, personnel and other forms of assistance in carrying out its mission on this great, largely underdeveloped island.

The Church in Southeast Indonesia

Nusa Tenggara, as this region is known to Indonesians, consists of two provinces comprising dozens of inhabited islands. The population —more than five and one-half million in the 1961 census—is divided into many different ethnic groups. Hinduism (on Bali and western Lombok), Islam (on eastern Lombok and Sumbawa), Roman Catholicism (on Flores and Portuguese Timor) and Protestant Christianity (on Indonesian Timor, Roti, Sawo, Solor and Alor) are the dominant religions. The indigenous religion (animism) is embraced on several of the islands, usually by a minority. Christians number approximately 1,135,000, nearly 20 percent of the population.

Both the pronounced cultural diversity of Southeast Indonesia and the relative lack of attention given to its development have characterized the region both under the colonial period and since independence. This means that transportation and communications are still extremely limited and inadequate and thus that church groups have not until recently been in close touch with one another. A close relation, however, has existed between the overseas missionary society and the church body it established.

We have already described the largest Protestant group, the Evangelical Christian Church of Timor. Moving westward, one finds the main concentration of Roman Catholics in Indonesia on the island of Flores, more than 600,000 strong. To the southwest lies the island of Sumba.

9 **The Sumba Christian Church (Geredja Kristen Sumba)** is the main Protestant body on this rather isolated island in eastern Nusa Tenggara Province. The population numbers around 300,000 at present and consists of several main indigenous groups in addition to people from other areas, mainly Sawu near Timor, who have settled on

Sumba over the last century. Sumba is wholly agricultural in character. There is some Islam, especially among the immigrants, but the main religion is animistic (belief in spirits).

It was not until the latter part of the nineteenth century that the colonial government paid any attention to Sumba, and then only to bring piracy and intergroup warfare under control. Only in 1906 did the island come under full colonial administration.

Christianity was first brought to Sumba by immigrants from Sawu island who had been settled in East Sumba between 1870 and 1875 by the Dutch resident of Timor, in an attempt to relieve the overcrowding on Sawu. They were ministered to by an Ambonese teacher-preacher.

Resident Esser, a devout Christian, requested the Netherlands Gereformeerd Missionary Society to send a missionary to Sumba, which was done in 1881. In 1883 there were 376 Sawonese Christians, but no Sumbanese had yet been baptized. Sumbanese society and culture were quite rigid and static. There were three distinct classes— the aristocracy, freemen and slaves—and little social intercourse between them. The ruling class strongly and effectively opposed Christianization. The first convert was baptized only in 1915, more than 35 years after Christianity was introduced. The spread of Dutch administration and an increase in the number and activity of Dutch missionaries gradually opened up the situation. The first congregation was established in 1916, primarily among the Sawonese. A school for evangelists was opened in 1924, which paved the way for advance among the Sumbanese. By 1940, there were 11 congregations with 6,500 members. A favorable factor in this growth was an agreement between the colonial government and the mission (in 1913) that responsibility for education was to be lodged wholly with the church.

Two developments presented a challenge to the mission in the 1930's. The first was the granting of government permission to the Roman Catholic Church to begin work in western Sumba. The second was a schism in the Gereformeerd Church itself over a question of church discipline, a matter regarded with great seriousness among Gereformeerd groups.

During the Japanese occupation the Sumba Church suffered greatly, but as in other places this experience both strengthened its organization and multiplied its members in all parts of the island. Presbyteries were established in the western, central and eastern regions of Sumba and in January, 1947, the Sumba Christian Church became autonomous. Today, 20 years later, the membership is more than 30,000, nearly 10 percent of the population. 44 ministers, 86 evangelists and

more than 200 evangelistic assistants are at work, and more than a
thousand persons presented themselves for baptism in the early months
of 1967.

In the social and educational fields the Sumba Church maintains a
Christian Hospitals Foundation and a Christian Schools Foundation.
The latter operates 140 primary schools, eight middle schools and
training schools for regular and religious teachers. A new agricultural
training center is also being built, and an agricultural missionary from
the Netherlands Gereformeerd Churches has recently arrived to help
develop this ministry.

10 **The Bali Protestant Christian Church (Geredja Kristen Protestan Bali)** is one of the youngest and smallest church bodies in
Indonesia. It also has the unique distinction of having been autonomous from the beginning, never dependent on foreign mission bodies.

Bali is frequently called "the isle of the gods." It is the only remaining area in Indonesia where Hinduism lives, and the traditional
religion (Bali-Hindu) permeates every sphere of life. Two million
people inhabit this small island, whose social and cultural life is richly
creative and intimately related to the 15,000 village temples and fre-
quent religious festivals. Bali is known throughout Indonesia, indeed
throughout the world, for its attractive dance, music, drama, painting
and woodcarving.

The first attempt to introduce the gospel to Bali was made in 1866
by two missionaries from the Utrecht Society of Holland. After seven
years of labor one Balinese was baptized, but eight years later he
was involved in the murder of the missionary. So the Dutch colonial
government closed Bali to missionary work.

Again in 1929 a Chinese bookseller of the Christian and Missionary
Alliance was permitted to preach among the Chinese on Bali. He
was so persuasive in his witness that several score Balinese asked to be
baptized. When a C.M.A. missionary baptized 113 Balinese in November, 1932, causing a general outcry against Christianity, the authorities withdrew permission for the C.M.A. to work in Bali. The opposition arose from several sources. Artists, anthropologists and
tourism promoters did not wish Balinese religious and cultural life
disturbed. The Balinese ruling groups did not wish to see any
pluralism in society. The colonial government desired to placate one
and all so as to reduce their problems to a minimum.

Dr. Hendrik Kraemer, however, the Dutch missionary statesman, wisely suggested that the East Java Church supply Javanese evangelists to serve in Bali. This produced promising results in the next few years. By 1938-1940 the first training course for evangelists was held, with the result that when the war came the church in Bali was able to survive because it was not dependent on anyone outside Bali. In 1943, it sent a minister to the East Java Church headquarters to be ordained so there would be a Balinese minister qualified to administer the sacraments. This was urgent, for the church had continued to grow. The most severe test, however, came after the Japanese surrender when Bali plunged into the storm of national revolution. The stand of Balinese Christians for national independence, despite their past ties with the Dutch church, gained them understanding and support from Balinese non-Christians. Thus after the independence struggle, with its attendant violence, the church found itself in a rapidly changing Bali.

In recent years the Protestant Church of Bali has turned its attention increasingly to the larger mission on the island. It has opened schools and hostels with assistance from the United Church of Christ in the United States and the Netherlands Reformed Church. It administered relief supplies contributed by churches around the world to minister to the thousands of Balinese made homeless by the tragic 1963 eruption of Mount Agung. And more recently it has cooperated with the Interchurch Aid Committee of the Council of Churches in several economic development projects on the island. The 1967 estimate was 6,900 members served by 17 ordained pastors in 32 local congregations. A great though difficult task lies ahead of this humble yet impressive young Balinese church.

Other Protestant groups working in Nusa Tenggara include the Christian and Missionary Alliance (in Bali, Lombok, Sumbawa, Roti, Flores and Alor) and the Pentecostals. In the eastern area, a Regional Council of Churches, including the Timor and Sumba Churches, was established in 1959.

FOOTNOTES

1. Cf. Stephen C. Neill, *Colonialism and Christian Missions*. London: Lutterworth Press, 1966, Chapter 6. For the historical in this and following chapters, the writer has relied heavily on Th. Müller-Krüger, *Sedjarah Geredja di Indonesia* (History of the Church in Indonesia). Djakarta: Badan Penerbit Kristen, 1959.

2. Cf. Th. Müller-Krüger, *Indonesia Raya*. Bad Salzuflen: MBK Verlag, 1966, pp. 117 ff.

3. Cf. Frank L. Cooley, "A Church Reformed and Reforming," *International Review of Missions*, Vol. LI, 1962, pp. 26-32.

5 The Churches of Sumatra and Kalimantan

SUMATRA AND THE NEARBY ISLANDS HAVE a population of 17,350,000 (93 per square mile). Five of the Council's member churches in this area have a combined membership of 1,141,000, or 6.7 percent of the population. The region is important in Indonesia's economy because of the large production of exportable agricultural commodities (rubber, coffee, peppers and tea) and minerals (petroleum and tin). Most of the congregations are in the villages, but many cities also have Christian communities. The smallest number of Christians are found in Atjeh and West Sumatra provinces, which are almost solidly Islamic.

Three of the five churches are among the Batak people, who occupy the Tapanuli region of North Sumatra. There are at least five distinct groups of Bataks, closely related ethnically but having some language and religious differences. The Mandailing and Angkola Bataks in South Tapanuli are largely Islamic. The Bataks to the north are more mixed—Christian, Islamic and indigenous (animistic) in religion. The Bataks are a vigorous, aggressive people seeking advance in various fields. This drive has taken many of them beyond their own borders in pursuit of better farm lands and of increased commercial, industrial, educational, political and military opportunities in the nation's life.

11 The Batak Protestant Christian Church (Huria Kristen Batak Protestan), among the Toba Bataks, is the largest single church body in Indonesia. It has a history of slightly over 100 years.

The Christian community in Tapanuli has resulted almost entirely from missionary activity of the Rhenish Missionary Society from Germany. Following unsuccessful attempts by the English Baptists in the 1820's, the American Congregationalists (whose first and only missionaries to Indonesia, Henry Lyman and Samuel Munson, were killed by the Bataks in 1834), the Netherlands Bible Society and, through its efforts, the Rhenish Missionary Society finally established work in South Tapanuli. The first converts came in 1861, from Islam. Dr. Ludwig Nommensen, the "Apostle to the Bataks," began a lifetime of work in this difficult but rewarding field in 1862. He died in 1918, after serving 56 years among the Bataks, from 1881 to 1918 as Ephorus or head of the church.

Progress was slow but steady between 1862 and 1881. Dutch colonial control of the region, established only after 1876, brought a larger measure of order and security and aided missionary efforts. A strong mass movement into Christianity began in 1883, and for 20 years the evangelization of the Toba Bataks proceeded rapidly. By the first decade of the twentieth century it was already spilling outside their boundaries into the Simalungun and Karo Batak regions as well as to the east coast areas, to which Batak farmers had emigrated. This spiritual revolution made a profound mark, establishing the church as one of the most prominent institutions in Batak society and identifying Toba Batak with Christianity.

Several features of the Batak Church's development stand out in contrast to the churches already described. These are due partly to Nommensen's genius as a missionary statesman, partly to the Rhenish Missionary Society background, quite different from the state church, and partly to distinctive characteristics of the Batak people.

First, the evangelization of Batak-land was carried out from the beginning by coordinated efforts according to a fixed plan, making full use of indigenous workers as soon as they could be trained. The first training school for Batak evangelists was established in 1868, within the first decade; and over the years the preparation of Batak personnel for the work of the church in local congregations, schools, hospitals and clinics and other service ministries received constant emphasis.

Another notable feature was the fixing in 1881 of a form of church order, only 20 years after the first Bataks were baptized. This enabled the church to grow strong in organization as well as in size. The General Synod was led by German missionaries up until 1940, when they were interned because of World War II. But for a long time there had developed pressures, partly due to nationalism and partly to healthy growth of the church, to bring the church wholly under Batak leadership. The Batak Church achieved autonomy in 1930, the first Indonesian church to do so. From 1940 it was wholly self-governing, self-supporting and self-propagating. This was the natural and inevitable result of Nommensen's and the Rhenish mission's policies, even though the missionaries were slow and reluctant to turn the church over to Batak leadership.

A third characteristic was the early missionary outreach by the Batak church itself. In 1900 an organization was formed to send evangelists to the Samosir, Simalungun and Karo areas. It was reorganized as the Batak mission in 1921 and was again adapted to meet the new situation after independence. Most recently the Batak Church has cooperated with other Sumatran churches in meeting the new opportunities following the 1965 coup.

In a variety of ways the Batak Church has developed a life and style of its own. It is an ethnic church in which the Batak language, Batak *adat* (custom and law) and Batak identity play a strong role. It is a singing church of unusual dimensions, though most of the hymns and choral numbers consist of Western tunes with the words translated into Batak language. There are strong women's and youth organizations as well as a number of types of social service outreach to meet special needs.

After the war, facing the need to rebuild and meet the new situation of independence and rapid social development, the Batak Church formulated its own confession and was accepted in 1953 as a member of the Lutheran World Federation. In the same year relations with the Rhenish Missionary Society were reestablished, with the latter sending missionaries to serve with the Batak Church. These ecumenical relations have made possible the founding in 1954 of Nommensen University, one of the earliest institutions of higher learning established by a religious body in Indonesia.

Unfortunately, mention must also be made of certain divisions or schisms within the Batak Church that seem to result from wholly nontheological factors, especially from tensions between various political, kinship and social groupings among the Batak people. In 1930 a nationalistic group desiring a complete break with Western influences in the church established the *Huria Kristen Batak*. After the revolution (1945) another much larger schism occurred and *Huria Kristen Indonesia* was established, but within the last year encouraging progress toward reconciliation has been reported. In 1963 a more serious division occurred in connection with the relation between the Batak Church and Nommensen University. Several leaders of the university who had been trained abroad, impatient with the traditional, parochial spirit of the leadership of the Batak Church, broke away and established the Protestant Christian Church of Indonesia (*Geredja Kristen Protestan Indonesia*). Various efforts have been made to reconcile the two groups, but to date little hope of early success is indicated.

The Batak Church at present has a constituency of more than 800,000, organized into 1,300 congregations with 220 ordained ministers in 11 districts.

12 The Simalungun Protestant Christian Church (Geredja Kristen Protestan Simalungun) considers its birthday to be September 3, 1903, the date on which the first Rhenish missionary settled among the Simalungun people.* Despite considerable efforts, the first 25 years saw only 900 baptisms and the establishment of 31 congregations. The contrast between the remarkable growth in the Toba Batak region and the slow growth in the neighboring Simalungun Batak region is probably caused by the fact that the Rhenish Mission used the Toba language in both the churches and the schools in the Simalungun region. Not until the Simalungun dialect began to be used, under strong pressure from the first Simalungun Christian leaders, did the rate of church growth increase. During the 1930's the preparation of materials in Simalungun began to arouse the tribal consciousness and associate Christianity with the Simalungun people. In 1940 the church, still controlled by the Toba Batak Church, counted 5,700 members and 60 congregations.

The Simalunguns' pressure for autonomy grew out of a conviction that evangelization would progress much faster if Simalungun culture and identity could be deeply touched by Christianity. But this argument was rejected by the Batak Church. Nevertheless, at the beginning of the Japanese occupation, after the Rhenish missionaries were interned, a Simalungun district of the Batak Church was established.

*I am indebted throughout this account for material supplied by the Reverend J. Depperman of the Rhenish Mission.

The wisdom and timeliness of this development is borne out by the notably increased rate of growth during the trying period of war and revolution (1940-1950). Now, for practical purposes on its own, there developed in the Simalungun Church a lay movement called "Witnesses for Christ," which took the gospel effectively to increasing numbers of Simalunguns, who were by then looking for a firmer ground than the old beliefs could provide. By the time the Rhenish missionaries returned in 1952, on the invitation of the Simalungun leaders, the church had grown to 21,600 members in 90 congregations, an increase of 290 percent in 12 years.

This experience substantially affected the views of the Batak Church on Simalungun autonomy. Freeing the church for its missionary task to at least 300,000 Simalungun people, of whom two-thirds still hold to the old tribal beliefs, was no longer seen as a matter of schism. So, in 1963, the Batak Protestant Christian Church declared the Simalungun Church to be independent. The following year the Simalungun Protestant Christian Church was accepted into membership in the Indonesia Council of Churches and the Lutheran World Federation. It continues to enjoy close cooperation with the Rhenish Mission. It also continues to manifest rapid growth (another 288 percent in the last 15 years), now registering 85,257 members in 208 congregations, served by 33 ordained ministers, five evangelists and 17 Bible women. This wide-open missionary situation requires and is forging more and closer cooperation among the churches in Sumatra.

13 The Karo Batak Protestant Church (Geredja Batak Karo Protestan) serves the most northerly group of Bataks. The people are primarily farmers with a tribal religion. Out of a total population of roughly 450,000, the Karo Church numbers nearly 50,000 or slightly more than 10 percent. Islam and Roman Catholicism are its major competitors for the allegiance of the remaining "animists."

The Karo Church has manifested remarkable growth in the years since World War II and the Indonesian revolutionary struggle (1945-1949). In 1940, after 50 years of work by the Netherlands Missionary Society, there were only 5,000 members. By 1946 the number had grown to 30,000. Since then, particularly after October, 1965, mass conversions have added more than 20,000 new members.

There are reasons for the slow start. First, the original request for missionary work in the region came from large Dutch-owned plantations, which encroached on the fertile lands of the Karo Bataks and aroused their opposition. The Dutch hoped that the Christianization of the Karo people would make them more docile under exploitation! So they were willing to underwrite the missionary program until 1930.

Second, instead of cooperating with the Rhenish Mission at work among the Toba Bataks and using Batak evangelists, the Netherlands Missionary Society appointed a Dutch missionary, Dr. H. C. Kruyt, who came with four Minahasan evangelists.

A third reason was timing. In contrast to the Toba area where evangelization preceded modernization, in the Karo area the missionary efforts followed the advance of secularization occasioned by development in the region.

National independence and church autonomy, plus the dynamic developments since 1945, greatly altered this situation, with the resulting church growth. This supports the observation by the moderator of the Synod of the Karo Church in 1959 that the Christian church had already taken root among the Karo people. Before the most recent spurt, the 30,000 members were found in 52 congregations served by eight ordained ministers. An increase of 25,000 members within a year and a half (June, 1966–November, 1967) means that the number of congregations has risen correspondingly. The Karo Church has issued an urgent appeal for immediate assistance, especially for personnel, from neighbor churches in Sumatra and Indonesia for help in assimilating the continuing growth in numbers. The response gives hope that ecumenical advance in mission in the Karo region will continue to expand.

14 **The Nias Protestant Christian Church (Banua Niha Keriso Protestan)**, with 225,000 members in 354 congregations, is the second largest church in Sumatra. Its territory encompasses the island of Nias and the smaller neighboring islands lying off the west coast of Sumatra opposite Tapanuli. Because of its geographic isolation and the late arrival of Dutch colonial government, Nias is less developed than the other areas of Sumatra.

The coming of Christianity and the growth of the church in Nias are in many respects similar to that of Tapanuli, for it was the Rhenish Missionary Society that undertook the task. The first missionary to enter Nias, the Rev. Mr. Denninger, arrived in 1865, settling in Gunung Sitoli, the main town and the only seat of Dutch colonial authority in the island at that time. It was not until 1874 that the first baptisms occurred, hence Easter Day, 1874 is celebrated as the

beginning of the Nias Church's history. The following statistics show
the growth of the church on Nias.

1874—first baptisms, 9 persons
1890—3 congregations with 906 Christians, after 25 years
1900—11 congregations with 5,000 Christians
1915—14 congregations with 20,000 Christians, after 50 years
1921—62,000 Christians
1940—135,000 Christians, after 75 years
1965—205,000 Christians, after 100 years

Two things are revealed by these figures. First, the early progress
was slow, only 5,000 Christians after 35 years, most of these between
1890 and 1900. Several reasons account for this. Geographic isolation
made communication difficult, and kinship ties tended to make village
communities self-contained units. Security and order had not yet been
established throughout the island by the Dutch. The heavy weight of
tradition (adat) was as yet unchallenged. After 1900, however, the
Dutch government established security and opened roads to most parts
of the island, and evangelization proceeded faster.

Second, in 1916 a great spiritual movement, fangesa dôdô, broke
out, leaving an indelible mark on the Nias Church. It was a movement
of mass conversion accompanied by widespread public confession of
personal sin and a sense of liberation and redemption, followed by
vigorous Christian witness. Place after place experienced this movement, which lasted for nine years. There were excesses arising from the
great outpouring of emotion. Some gifts of the Spirit were misused,
and certain Pentecostal phenomena came to be valued as ends in
themselves. But by and large this first wave of fangesa dôdô was
positive. It raised up many native evangelists, who after receiving some
training were assigned to lead village congregations. It gave an unusual
dimension of personal spiritual experience to many Nias Christians.

There were other waves of this same phenomenon, the most pronounced coming just after World War II, but they brought no positive
fruits to the life of the church. In fact, in some cases they led to schism,
which is frequently an accompaniment of such Pentecostal phenomena.

In church organization and liturgy, developments in the Nias
Church paralleled those in the Batak Church. The first native min-
isters were graduated in 1906 from a recently opened training school in
Ombôlata. By 1940, when the German missionaries were interned, the
Nias Church was able to function under its own leadership. The first
Synod meeting was held in 1936, four years before the election of the
first Nias pastor to head the church. The Rev. A. Harefa served as

Ephorus from 1940 to 1950. Relations with the Rhenish Mission remained cordial, and after 1951 missionaries were again invited to work with the Nias Church.

Three problems among those faced by the Nias Church are mentioned here. First, the relative isolation of the region, caused by geography, has hindered the development of close relations with other churches in Indonesia, as well as the growth of the Nias Church itself. Second, like the Batak Church the Nias Church has had to struggle with the heavy weight of custom and tradition (*adat isti adat*) on social life in Nias. For example, the impossibly high bride price has caused problems in marriage relations and encouraged moral irregularities. Third, the *fangesa dôdô* background and the continuing "spiritual movements" have made it difficult to maintain church unity. Competition has come from without, too; Adventist and Roman Catholic missions were established after 1950, when the Christianization of the Nias people was nearly complete.

15　**The Indonesia Methodist Church (Geredja Methodis Indonesia)** has grown from American efforts begun in 1903 on Java after contacts had been established by former pupils of American Methodist English schools in Malaya and Singapore. Schools, especially English schools, were a strong emphasis in the program until an Indonesian government ordinance prohibiting foreign language schools for Indonesian citizens was promulgated in 1959. As a result of the depression of 1929 and the consequent retrenchment of mission programs, the Methodists withdrew from Java and concentrated available resources on Sumatra.

The two main centers of Methodist work were the region around Medan in the north and the region around Palembang in the south. At the beginning the efforts of missionaries were focused on the Chinese in the cities and large towns. But later on work developed among the Bataks—Simalungun and Toba—who came to the coastal areas in search of a better livelihood. This led eventually to a problem of relationships with the Batak Church, but it has been solved in a good spirit of cooperation. The Methodist Church contributed both funds and personnel to the Theological Faculty of Nommensen University in Pematang Siantar and uses that school for training some of its pastors. The Methodist Church in Indonesia is found primarily in urban situations. In addition to congregations and schools, it operates a small printing plant that serves the Sumatra churches.

In 1922 North Sumatra became a separate mission, and in 1925 the North Sumatran Mission Conference was organized. Just after World War II there were approximately 60 congregations enrolling 3,000 members, served by 40 ordained and local preachers. Since then the church has grown rapidly. Today the Indonesia Methodist Church numbers 40,000 members in 199 congregations, but since there are only 35 ordained pastors, many congregations must be served by local preachers.

Until recently this Methodist organization was part of a church body located outside Indonesia. During the Indonesian-Malaysian "confrontation," the Methodist group in Sumatra decided to choose an autonomous status. This was accepted by the parent body, and in 1964 the Methodist Church of Indonesia came into being. It is self-governing yet preserves cordial cooperative relations with the Board of Missions of The United Methodist Church in the U.S.A. This new status could lead the Methodist Church to much closer relations with sister churches in Indonesia as well as to more active participation in the Council of Churches.

To round out the picture of Christianity in the Sumatra region it should be mentioned that the Nias Church is engaged in missionary work on the Batu Islands while the Batak Church mission has given help to the struggling and declining population on Enggano. Both the Batak Church and Rhenish Mission have given assistance for work on the Mentawei Islands, where there is already an autonomous Christian church, the *Paamian Kristen Protestan Mentawei*, with a membership of approximately 35,000.

Finally it will be recalled that the Western Indonesia Protestant Church has congregations in several of the larger cities in Sumatra, notably Medan, Palembang and Padang, and has recently cooperated with other Sumatran churches in their mission to the region.

The Church on Kalimantan

16   The Kalimantan Evangelical Church (Geredja Kalimantan Evangelis) is the largest Protestant church on this second largest of the Indonesian islands. The Indonesian part of Borneo, as it is known in the West, is divided into four provinces with a population of four and one-half million, concentrated in the southern and western regions. The Dajaks comprise the main ethnic group, aside from the Malays

who have settled in the coastal towns. Topographic conditions—wet lowlands traversed by many rivers providing the arteries of communication—accentuated the development of many subtribes of Dajaks, who now show marked differences in language, tradition and identity. The moderator of the church recently summarized Kalimantan's main characteristics as "rivers, swamps, mosquitoes and jungle forests." Dutch rule did not come to the interior of the island until the beginning of the twentieth century. There has been little economic development of the region. As for religious faith, nearly three million are Muslims; one million embrace the primal religion called *Kaharingan;* and about 300,000, or 7 percent of the population, are Christians.

After hearing the optimistic reports of a British Baptist visitor, the Rhenish Missionary Society decided to open work on Borneo in 1836. The history of the Kalimantan Church is usually divided into four phases: 1) 1836-1859, 2) 1866-1906, 3) 1906-1935, and 4) 1935 to the present.

In the period from 1836 to 1859, the church spread to the lower reaches of several of the large rivers, where Islam was already dominant. The progress of evangelization was very slow because of opposition from Islam and because the Dajaks, holding strongly to traditional practices such as headhunting, were hard to reach. Efforts such as redeeming slaves and providing education were undertaken, but visible results were infinitesimal. During this 20-year period only 261 persons were baptized. Nevertheless the Rhenish Mission was not discouraged and in 1858 planned several new enterprises to extend the work. In 1859, however, the Hidajat rebellion radically altered the picture. This rebellion, though primarily anti-European and political, profoundly affected the infant church. Four missionaries were killed and all missionary activity was halted by the colonial authorities.

After seven years, in 1866, the Dutch government again granted permission to Rhenish missionaries to return and begin work; at first only in areas near Dutch military posts. Progress was slow but the work expanded toward the upper reaches of the Murong, Kapuas, Kahajan and Barito Rivers into what is now Central Kalimantan, where Islam had not yet penetrated. The total number of Christians by 1906 was 2,000, after 70 years of missionary activity.

The third period, 1906-1935, saw slow but steady advance both in area and intensity of missionary efforts. By 1925, when the number of Christians had increased to 5,400, there were 50 congregations, 19 evangelists and 77 teachers under the direction of 14 missionaries. In that same year the Rhenish Missionary Society found it necessary to transfer its work in Kalimantan to the Basel Mission in Switzerland. This did not greatly affect the Kalimantan Church because the two European societies were similar in background and emphasis. Leadership training was expanded. The colonial government increased its emphasis on health and educational services, and consequently more teachers, nurses, evangelists and ministers were trained. In 1935 the Dajak Evangelical Church, complete with a Synod organization and polity, was born. At this time too work began among the Chinese communities in the coastal towns. Awareness also grew that the Muslims represented not only a competitor and a problem, but also a field for which the church must assume responsibility.

Shortly after the Dajak Evangelical Church was established, Japanese occupation necessitated the withdrawal of all missionaries and the young church was on its own. Like all other churches in Indonesia, it not only survived the ordeal but grew stronger under indigenous leadership and self-support. In 1953 Swiss missionaries were invited to return to work primarily in leadership training projects, particularly the Theological School in Bandjarmasin, capital city of South Kalimantan. At this time the name of the church was changed to the Evangelical Church of Kalimantan, symbolizing the fact that the entire island is the church's mission field.

Today this church has 67,667 members, 300 congregations organized into 37 districts, 66 ordained ministers and 60 evangelists, and half a dozen overseas missionaries. In addition to cooperation with the Basel Missionary Society in Central and South Kalimantan, a new tie with the Netherlands Missionary Council will enable more concentrated work in West Kalimantan.

Reports indicate that "the door for the gospel is wide open in Kalimantan at present." For some years now about 2,000 non-Christians have been baptized annually. Islam and *Kaharingan* (indigenous religion) are the two great challengers, the former nearly three times as large as the latter and much tougher.

Until recently there has been little cooperation between various Protestant groups working in Kalimantan. Within the last two years, however, a Regional Council of Churches has been formed with five members: the Evangelical Church and the Gospel Spreading Church, which are Kalimantan-based bodies; and three whose Synod headquarters are elsewhere, the Western Indonesia and Batak Churches, which have only a few congregations in the coastal towns of Kalimantan, and the Bethel Full Gospel Church, a Djakarta-based Pentecostal body with numerous congregations in Central Kalimantan. The latter undertakes vigorous evangelistic activities, while the Western Indonesia and Batak Churches largely care for their own. Cooperative activities of the members of the Regional Council have been limited to date mostly to worship services and special occasions. But their cooperation in health and educational services at a government development project is an example of what is possible in ecumenical witness and service.

Outside the Regional Council, a number of other church bodies or overseas missionary groups are at work, such as the Christian and Missionary Alliance, the World Evangelization Crusade, the Go Ye Fellowship, Conservative Baptists and the Regions Beyond Missionary Union, mostly in West Kalimantan. These cooperate among themselves but not with other groups. Their sole emphasis is personal evangelism and they are still largely foreign staffed, directed and financed. Together they number possibly 100,000 members.

In 1966 there were 33,779 Roman Catholics in Kalimantan. This church is working vigorously to expand its numbers and so presents a strong challenge to the Kalimantan Church and other Protestant groups.

The most urgent needs in facing its opportunities are more and better trained leaders and help in overcoming the communications problem. The Kalimantan Evangelical Church welcomes, in fact has urged, assistance from sister churches in Indonesia and overseas.

17 **The Gospel Spreading Christian Church (Geredja Kristen Pemantjar Indjil)** is one of the most recent (1962) and smallest churches to become a member of the Council of Churches. This church is located in an isolated area of Northeast Kalimantan, and it may have developed out of Christian and Missionary Alliance work in that area. The most recent statistics show 10,200 members, 41 congregations and four ordained pastors. The Kalimantan Church has lent them a pastor and has made the facilities of its Theological School in Bandjarmasin available to train their workers.

6 The Churches on Sulawesi

SULAWESI (FORMERLY CELEBES) IS THE large octopus-shaped island to the east of Kalimantan. It has a population of around eight million, spread on the average of 100 per square mile. About 15 percent, or 1,150,000 are Christian. Of these, nearly a million are in eight church bodies that are members of the Indonesia Council of Churches. Islam is very strong in South Sulawesi. The other areas contain Christians, Muslims and some groups that still embrace primal tribal beliefs.

Some areas of Sulawesi, such as the Minahasa region, are quite highly developed economically, socially and culturally. Yet on the whole, land communications are poor, so that most movement of goods and people takes place by sea.

The geographic features of Sulawesi account partly for the remarkable variety among the people. In this respect it is one of the most diverse regions of Indonesia, a fact that has been significant for the general development of the region as well as for the spread of Christianity. Nearly one-fourth of the member churches of the Council of Churches are on Sulawesi. In 1953, of the non-Roman religious bodies registered with the Ministry of Religion, Sulawesi had 25 out of 165, or 15 percent. Only Java had more.

The Minahasan and Sangir-Talaud churches have already been

pictured in the description of the Indonesia Protestant Church. The others, which are to be introduced here, resulted from missionary activity, begun mostly in the nineteenth century.

18   The Bolaang Mongondow Evangelical Christian Church (Geredja Masehi Indjili Bolaang Mongondow) is neighbor to the Minahasa Church. The area, lying west-southwest of Minahasa, was Islamized during the latter half of the nineteenth century. There had been some Christians there during the East India Company period when Bolaang Mongondow was administered as a part of Minahasa, but because of neglect by the Company church they all slipped back into the tribal religion or became Muslims. Quite understandably Christianity moved across the border into Bolaang Mongondow as Minahasans settled there to work empty lands. But the colonial government refused permission for missionary work in Bolaang Mongondow until the beginning of the twentieth century, by which time the process of Islamization had already gone far. Today 80 percent of the population, numbering around 100,000, embraces Islam.

The Dutch Reformed Missionary Society sent its first missionary into the area in 1904, now celebrated as the year in which the church was founded. By that time 1,500 Minahasan Christians were there, which created problems. The Minahasans had been Christian for several generations, and Christianity had become traditional with them. They required a ministry appropriate to their condition. The Bolaang Mongondow members by contrast were new Christians living daily in confrontation with Islam. The needs of the two groups were thus quite different. Also the Malay language customarily used in the Minahasan Church was not familiar to the Bolaang Mongondow people; they needed a ministry in the vernacular. And there were other cultural differences between the two groups. Even today nearly five-sixths of the members of the Bolaang Mongondow Church are from Minahasa, only one-sixth being natives of Bolaang Mongondow. To further complicate the situation, in recent years 3,000 Balinese families, of whom a few are Christian, have transmigrated to Bolaang Mongondow and require the church's ministry.

The first Synod was organized in 1940, but the Evangelical Christian Church of Bolaang Mongondow, with headquarters in Kotamobagu, counts June 28, 1950 as the beginning of its autonomous period. During the Darul Islam and PERMESTA rebellions (1959-1962), almost all church property was destroyed and many villages burned.

In such an isolated region with almost no roads, rebuilding has been steady but slow.

The Bolaang Mongondow Church in 1967 reported 30,600 members in 95 congregations served by seven ordained ministers and 13 evangelists. The church operates nine elementary and five secondary schools, together with five polyclinics. Both educational and health work, as well as some new agricultural work, are being expanded as fast as resources and personnel become available. Church leaders report the same condition that obtains in most of the areas described thus far: "The harvest indeed is plentiful, but the laborers are extremely few." The church has candidate ministers, teachers, nurses and doctors in training. It has requested help from other churches. To date it has cooperative working relations with only the Netherlands Reformed Church. Bolaang Mongondow is host to the North Sulawesi Regional Council of Churches, whose program is only beginning to develop. It has asked this Regional Council to think about a solution to the problems created by the entrance of "sects" and other noncooperating groups into its field (six so far, in addition to the Roman Catholics). The Evangelical Christian Church of Bolaang Mongondow is keenly aware of its isolation and the need for better communication and cooperation with the other churches in Indonesia.

19 The Central Sulawesi Christian Church (Geredja Kristen Sulawesi Tengah) is located in the northern portion of Central Sulawesi among the Toradja people. (Toradja is a general name applied to four of the ethnic groups inhabiting the central part of Sulawesi.) Two other churches are found among the Toradjas living further south. The Central Sulawesi Church actually covers a larger area and probably includes more varied groups than either of the other two Toradja churches, even though it is not the largest.

This church is especially interesting because it is the fruit of a careful plan for the Christianization of all the people in the region. Its early history is largely the story of two remarkable missionaries from the Netherlands Missionary Society, Dr. Albert C. Kruyt and Dr. N. Adriani. Kruyt's original destination was the Gorontalo region to the north, but since the Islamization of this area was nearly complete by the time of his arrival in 1891, Kruyt soon concluded that it would be wiser to move to North Central Sulawesi, where Islam had not yet penetrated. Being the son of a Dutch missionary in East Java, he was convinced of the crucial importance of presenting the gospel in language and cultural forms acceptable to the people. Thus for 17 years Kruyt and Adriani studied the languages, customs, religions and ways of thinking of the Toradja peoples. In the process, they compiled voluminous writings on the ethnology of the region, which have been given high praise by other anthropologists.

A second conviction of Kruyt's and Adriani's was that these people should come into the Christian community in groups, by whole villages where possible, to avoid isolating new Christians from their own society and culture. This strategy, carried out in an area where Dutch administration was just being established, where means of communication were being developed and schools were being opened, resulted in the rapid Christianization of the tribes in the region. In a period of 30 years, beginning with the baptism on Christmas Day, 1909, of 180 people near Poso, the mass movement spread to all the areas around the Poso Lake and to the east as far as Luwuk and Banggai islands. Evangelists and teachers from Minahasa were brought in to help before the establishment of schools to prepare Toradja workers. A course for training evangelists and ministers was opened in Tentena in 1940. But since these efforts could not produce the large number of teachers, evangelists and ministers required by such a rapidly growing church, there was inadequate instruction and pastoral care in many areas.

The autonomous Central Sulawesi Christian Church was established in 1947 with the usual presbyterial-synodal pattern of organization. Today there are 126,467 members in 339 congregations served by 56 ordained ministers. No foreign missionaries have been working with the Central Sulawesi Church since 1961, though fraternal relations with the Netherlands Missionary Society continue. One of the biggest problems that this church faces, within its own region and in its relations with other churches, is extreme isolation. Both transportation and communications have made it exceedingly difficult for this church to remain or grow as one church. Fragmentation may continue until the development of the region progresses, a prospect not yet in sight.

20 **The Makale-Rantepao Toradja Christian Church (Geredja Kristen Toradja, Makale-Rantepao)** is both larger and younger than the Central Sulawesi Church. It grew from efforts of missionaries sent by the Dutch Christian Reformed Missionary Association. The first missionary, Van Loosdrecht, entered Toradja-land in 1913 but was later killed in a tribal rebellion against the Dutch. His murderer, who

died just a few years ago, was captured and after a prison term became
a Christian. Other missionaries were sent to Makale, Rongkong and
Palopo. Schools and teacher training courses were established, and a
hospital was built in the 1930's. By 1942 the membership was 40,000.

Immediately after World War II, the Synod of the Toradja Church
was organized and the period of autonomy began. The membership
of 75,000 in 1947 doubled by 1954, a growth so rapid that it was impossible to instruct and serve all the new congregations adequately,
despite vigorous efforts to train evangelists and teachers.

Problems, inherent in such rapid growth, were compounded by the
fierce persecution to which this Toradja Church was subjected by
fanatical Muslim elements from the Bugis area to the south. From the
earliest days Islamic rulers had raided this area to secure slaves and to
Islamize the population by force. This pressure increased after 1952,
with the disappointment of Islamic groups that Indonesia had not
been made an Islamic state. Christian villages were attacked, homes
and churches burned, people abducted and murdered. Government
protection was insufficient and the Darul Islam rebel units moved
freely about the region. Thousands of Toradja Christians fled as
refugees to more isolated areas to the north, and to the large towns and
cities in the south where government protection could be assured. The
church followed its people and provided ministry while they were in
exile.

After Darul Islam leaders were captured by government forces in
1964, the region's security was restored and it was again safe for
Christians to return to their villages and rebuild. The Toradja Church
faces a broad new opportunity, but it must have more personnel to
make the most of the present situation. Today the church has a
membership of more than 185,000 spread over 297 congregations served
by 43 ordained ministers, 20 gospel teachers and 200 lay elders. These
figures tell the story of both the needs and the opportunities this
gallant church faces.

21   The Mamasa Toradja Christian Church (Geredja Kristen
Toradja Mamasa) has a history nearly identical with that of its
neighbor, the Makale-Rantepao Toradja Church, except that there had
been some Christian work in this region by the Protestant Church of
Indonesia, the schools being staffed by Ambonese Christian teachers.
Missionary work was undertaken in 1929 by a Christian Reformed
group from the Netherlands. After five years there were 5,000 members,

and by 1954 nearly 30,000 Toradja people in this region had become Christian. The Mamasa Church, which became autonomous in 1948, also experienced intense persecution at the hands of Islamic and other political rebels, as did their neighbors to the east. The 1967 estimate reported 40,000 members in 135 congregations, presided over by seven ordained ministers.

Efforts to unite the three churches working among the Toradja people have been to no avail but remain alive. A report on the situation of the churches in Toradja-land in early 1967 concludes with these words: "Everywhere many people are receiving the good news of salvation. The important thing now is the nurture of the congregations and guidance of the Lord's sheep. We are confronted by a desperate shortage of personnel. Pray that the Lord may bless us by sending laborers to the place of his harvest."

22 The Southeast Sulawesi Protestant Church (Geredja Protestan Sulawesi Tenggara), like the churches just described, is a twentieth century development. The area it serves extends like a tentacle southeast from the part of Central Sulawesi we have just been considering. Islam of a quite militant kind is the dominant religion all around the coast, and primal religious belief still predominates inland. Before 1900 there was only one Christian congregation in the area, consisting of Ambonese and Minahasans and located in Kendari, the main town. But like other *Indisch Kerk* congregations belonging to the "fourth church" of that time, it did not engage in missionary outreach among local people.

In 1915, the Netherlands Missionary Society (*Nederlandsche Zendingsvereeniging*), already at work in West Java, began evangelistic activities in Southeast Sulawesi at Mowewe, then under the influence of the Bugis-Muslim rulers in Luwu. The first baptisms were performed in 1929, and the work expanded slowly throughout the region. Difficulties were always present, caused by the opposition of Islamic rulers to Christian work among the tribal people. By 1938, the Christian community numbered around 3,000.

During the Japanese occupation and the years immediately following the proclamation of Indonesian Independence, organized Islamic opposition increased, inflicting considerable suffering on the small, isolated Christian groups. Only in 1965 did the Indonesian government finally break the power of the Darul Islam rebel group that controlled Southeast Sulawesi for many years.

The reestablishment of public security and governmental authority has confronted the church with two new opportunities and difficulties. On the one hand, thousands of people formerly occupying rebel-held areas have recently left the jungle-covered hills and poured into towns and cities empty handed, both materially and spiritually. They represent an immediate object of witness and service for the church, but the church lacks resources to minister to them. Second, with normality beginning to return, there is a vigorous drive to develop the region. The church wants to participate actively in this development but is stymied again for lack of resources. The Interchurch Aid Commission of the Council of Churches has channeled some resources contributed by overseas churches to stimulate agricultural and transport development. Though the Southeast Sulawesi Church is very small (6,611 members, 32 congregations and 13 ordained ministers), its efforts have attracted notice and approval from both government and Muslims. But the church's leaders feel that if the church is slow to participate in the problems of the refugees and the developments that are currently urgent, it may well lose this timely opportunity for both witness and service. Their report, early in 1967, closes with the fervent hope that "the oneness of the Church will promptly become a reality so that the struggles of weak churches can quickly elicit responses from neighbor churches that are mature."

23 **The South Sulawesi Christian Church (Geredja Kristen Sulawesi Selatan)** works among the strongly Islamic and vigorous Buginese and Makassarese ethnic groups that inhabit the southern end of Sulawesi, especially the region around and to the south of the city of Makassar. Since for many hundreds of years this city has been the primary seaport for East Indonesia, the East India Company established congregations for its employees in the region during the latter part of the seventeenth century. But these were not missionary congregations that reached out to the Buginese and Makassarese people.

Twice, during the period from 1851 to 1864 and again from 1895 to 1905, the Netherlands Missionary Society attempted to establish a church among these people, but withdrew when there was no response whatever. A third attempt was made in 1933 when both the Protestant Church of Western Indonesia and three Christian Reformed congregations in Central and East Java sent missionaries to South Sulawesi, establishing schools and a hospital as well as direct evangelistic activities. This time there was some response, and the work progressed.

After the war the three groups pooled their resources and functioned through a united committee, which coordinated and directed the evangelistic, educational and medical activities. A school was opened in Makassar to train evangelists and itinerant booksellers (*colporteurs*). Work fanned out from six stations into three regions (Selajar Island, Wattang Soping and Makassar City). By 1967 this young church numbered 3,500 Christians, in 17 congregations with five ordained ministers. This is one of the few church bodies in Indonesia whose mission is exclusively among Muslims, and it is a most difficult and challenging field.

7 The Churches on Java

JAVA IS THE MOST POPULOUS REGION of Indonesia. Over seventy-seven million inhabitants spread across this island, at a density greater than 1,200 persons per square mile. It was the center of interest for the Dutch colonial regime after 1830 and is now the most developed region of Indonesia in transportation, communications, industry, education and urbanization.

There are three main ethnic groups on Java: the Javanese (51 million), who inhabit East and Central Java; the Sundanese (24 million), who occupy West Java; and the Chinese (two million), who have settled in the towns and cities throughout Java. At least 100,000 or 5 percent of the Chinese, 170,000 or 0.35 percent of the Javanese, and 15,000 or 0.074 percent of the Sundanese are Protestant Christians. These figures reveal how much smaller is the relative numerical strength of the Java Protestant community than in other areas.

24 **The East Java Christian Church (Geredja Kristen Djawi Wetan),** with the exception of the Western Indonesia Church, is the oldest church on Java. It has some distinctive qualities, among them the fact that from the beginning laymen have played a major role in the spread of the gospel and the growth of the church in East Java. It

was neither originally nor primarily the result of the work of foreign missionaries.

Developments during the first period of the East Java Church's history (1830-1848) suggest that quite a different situation might have evolved had the Dutch authorities permitted and encouraged missionary work among the Javanese. There were two favorable circumstances that could have accounted for a large response. One was that before 1800 Islam had not yet taken deep roots in Javanese society, especially in East Java where there is a strong mystical tendency that combines Hindu and animistic elements. The second was a characteristic Javanese culture pattern, *mentjari ngelmu,* the active search for a way or secret of life that will bring peace of mind and fulfilment. There was an attitude of openness and seeking that could have led to a positive response to the gospel.

Several persons and places figure prominently in this first period. The first was C. L. Coolen of Ngoro. His father was a Dutch military man and his mother a Javanese woman descended from the Mataram princes. He combined elements of the West, especially the independent, Christian spirit, with the mystical, symbolic, monistic spirit of the Javanese social and cultural patterns. This "Javanese Christianity" proved attractive to seeking Javanese because it did not involve a radical break with their own social and cultural milieu. It was from Coolen that men from Wiung, a village near Surabaja, found the *ngelmu* they were seeking and formed a group of Javanese Christians in their own village.

A contrasting development was taking place around a German watchmaker named Emde, who settled in Surabaja after being demobilized from the Dutch navy during the English period. Coming out of German pietism, Emde was deeply influenced by Joseph Kam in Surabaja on the latter's way to the Moluccas in 1816. He became the leader of an evangelical group in the Protestant Church congregation in Surabaja. Emde's approach, in contrast to Coolen's, emphasized a "westernized Christianity" which by imposing certain European patterns of life on new Christians separated them from the Javanese community and its culture. When the leaders of the Wiung group came to Emde to study Christianity further they agreed, despite the differences from what they had received from Coolen, to be baptized and accommodate their Javanese style of life. By 1845 the Protestant congregation in Surabaja had already baptized 220 Javanese, and Emde's group was giving strong support to a variety of missionary efforts in East Java.

Nevertheless, the real beginning of the church in East Java was not in the westernized atmosphere of the city, but in a rural setting where the Javanese could be themselves. A group of Javanese Christian pioneers, led by Paulus Tosari, cleared a tract of virgin jungle that was reportedly haunted to establish the Christian village of Modjowarno, which developed into the "mother congregation" of the East Java Church. Tosari was a Madurese who had accepted Christ under the influence of Coolen, Pak Dasimah (leader of the ten men of Wiung), and the Sidoardjo community of Günsch. Tosari provided the spiritual leadership for the Modjowarno development, which became the model for several other Christian villages established later. Thus Christianity was firmly rooted in East Java before the coming of Dutch missionaries.

In 1847-1848 the Netherlands Missionary Society dispatched Van Rhijn to undertake a survey of the Indies and formulate recommendations for the development of its work. After completing his survey, Van Rhijn, with great effort, persuaded the government to permit evangelistic work on Java. The Rev. J. E. Jellesma was the first missionary to settle in East Java, in 1849, inaugurating the second period in the East Java Church's history.

Jellesma moved from Surabaja to Modjowarno in 1851 and within a few years succeeded in the difficult task of bridging the wide gap between Coolen's "Javanese Christianity" and Emde's "Dutch Christianity." He persuaded the former to accept the sacraments and the latter to accept the principle that Javanese who became Christians were to remain Javanese. Before his death in 1858, Jellesma baptized 2,500 persons. Convinced that the gospel should be preached by Javanese, he began the training of young Javanese evangelists, first in his home and later in a school he established in Modjowarno. These evangelists were sent out to minister to new congregations. Jellesma's policies were continued by other Dutch missionaries, who followed the spread of the gospel and the expansion of the church by giving guidance and instruction as well as providing resources for "the equipping of the saints" in these missionary congregations.

A characteristic development during this period was the establishment of Christian villages, after the model at Modjowarno, in the area south from Malang to Djember and south of Kediri. Swaru, Sitiardjo, Peniwen, Lumadjang, Tundjungredjo, Tulungagung and Sumberagung, prominent Christian villages established by Javanese Christians between 1870 and 1910, became the backbone of the East Java Church.

As Javanese Christians began to move to the towns and cities after 1910, the church followed them and organized congregations in cities such as Malang (1920) and Surabaja (1930). Schools and hospitals followed and provided an important educational and service dimension of the ministry of the church.

This latter development in the East Java Church hastened the movement toward autonomy, and on December 11, 1931, the *Madjelis Agung*, or Synod, of the East Java Christian Church assumed full responsibility for leading and governing the church. An organizational pattern and polity suitable to the situation and needs of the church in East Java was created. Dutch missionaries continued to serve, but within the autonomous church. The Synod assumed responsibility for training lay leadership at the village level and for the theological education of ministers for the whole church. Balewyoto, the theological institute, was established in 1926 to prepare candidate ministers for a relevant confrontation of the Christian faith and Javanism. Dr. Schuurman prepared a textbook in dogmatics especially aimed at achieving this end, one of the few efforts to date to write Christian theology within Indonesian patterns of thought.

These developments helped prepare the church for the fiery trials it had to undergo during the Japanese occupation and the revolution. Japanese suspicions that Christians in East Java were collaborating with the Dutch resulted in the imprisonment and torture of many ministers. Some were killed when they refused to betray their church and their people. During the revolutionary period difficulties were even greater because of the large-scale military operations in the fierce struggle for independence. The forthright position of the church on the nationalist side interrupted for a time, and modified for all time, the relationship with the Netherlands Missionary Society. But throughout, the East Java Church continued to grow in numbers, in strength and in the respect of the people.

The East Java Church has been a missionary church from the beginning. In addition to its role in establishing the church on Bali in the 1930's, there has been continuing concern to take the gospel to the Islamic people of Madura, a heavily populated island lying off the north coast of East Java.

Especially since 1958 the missionary activity of the church, notably of local congregations, has increased markedly. The actual outreach is done by members of the missionary commission of the local congregation, largely laymen, who make use of family gatherings and festivals, Christian holidays and the like to hold evangelistic meetings in homes

of Christians to which all neighbors are invited. Since 1960 the church
has held each year a churchwide Proclamation of the Gospel Week,
seeking to reach every village in East Java.

Out of these efforts at least 1,000 adults per year were baptized between 1954 and 1965. In 1964 the East Java Church's membership
was 62,890, and the most recent estimate is 85,000. A recent report on
evangelism makes the following comments:

> After the September 30th Affair [abortive coup in 1965] . . . during
> July and August 1966 nearly 10,000 persons were baptized. Many think
> that these were people close to the Communist Party who came into the
> church simply out of a desire to seek protection. This assumption is too
> simple. As a matter of fact, such large numbers are not only because of
> the September 30 Affair, but even more represent candidates who prior
> to that date were "Nicodemuses" attracted in preceding years by the
> evangelistic campaigns of the Church. They were afraid to come in be-
> fore but the September 30th Affair moved them to wait no longer. Many
> among this large number came from Islam and Javanese mysticism.
>
> To speak about these new developments in evangelism forces us also
> to speak about how the many new groups are to be nurtured, and also
> how the structures and forms of the Church can face this situation which
> has confronted it so quickly and in such a massive fashion. . . . There
> are not enough ministers able to stand as strong pillars in the midst of
> these new groups. And without them, it will not be strange if these
> groups in time retreat. . . .

In Central Java there are three churches, each with a different
missionary society connection and ecclesiastical background. Two of
them are members of the Council of Churches.

25 **The Java Christian Churches (Geredja-Geredja Kristen Djawa)**
have a *Gereformeerde* (Christian Reformed) background. But missionaries did not play a major role until the twentieth century. The
beginnings of the church in Central Java came from evangelistic efforts
of individual Dutch Christians, like Mr. Keuchenius; Indo-European
Christians, like Mrs. Philips-Steven; and Javanese Christians, like
Sadrach. On October 10, 1858, two men and seven women from Banjumas were baptized in the Protestant church in Semarang, after
walking 42 hours to reach the church. Small groups of believers formed
in Tegal, Purworedjo, Banjumas and other towns. Sadrach, a Javanese
from Djapara, on the north coast, journeyed to various centers of

Christian activity from Modjowarno in East Java to Djakarta in West Java, where he was finally baptized in 1867. In 1869 he joined Mrs. Philips-Steven in Purworedjo and, after her death, became the leader of a movement of Javanese Christians that by 1873 already numbered more than 2,000. Like Coolen before him, Sadrach sought to develop a Javanese form of Christianity that would not involve a radical break with Javanese culture.

When the first missionaries of the Netherlands Gereformeerd Missionary Society entered Central Java in the late 1880's, there were already 9,000 Christians in scores of congregations under the overall leadership of Sadrach. The missionaries sought to take over leadership and develop the indigenous Christian movement according to Gereformeerd theology and polity. Sadrach was prepared to welcome them and cooperate, but was understandably unwilling to turn leadership over to them, even though he was not an ordained minister. One of the missionaries, Wilhelm, did work with him as an "adviser" and teacher in the congregation in a mutually satisfactory way.

But in 1891 the Christian Reformed missions inspector in Indonesia ruled that the missionaries must work separately from Sadrach's movement. Thus the opportunity of building on a broad indigenous foundation was lost, and the missionaries had to start from the beginning. Sadrach's movement, cut off from ecumenical contacts, continued as a sect in the eyes of both government and missionaries. When Sadrach died the movement came under the leadership of his adopted son, Jotham. After 1930, members began to join the congregations being established by missionary efforts.

The missionaries made the cities rather than the villages the base of mission in Central Java. In characteristic Gereformeerde style, local congregations in Holland established ties with the local congregations in Java under the care of their missionaries. It was the congregation that carried responsibility for mission. Educational, medical and social work was emphasized as a tool of evangelism. By 1937 there were 159 elementary and 50 secondary schools. Among the latter, the Dutch school in Solo for training teachers exerted a wide and lasting influence in developing Christian schools. By the same year, nine hospitals served more than 3,000 inpatients and many more outpatients. Literature production and distribution has always been a special emphasis in the Central Java Church.

By 1938 there were 55 local congregations, 14 of them served by Javanese pastors. The training of teachers and evangelists had begun in 1906 in Jogjakarta. The first Javanese minister, Sopater, was ordained in 1926. Though these local congregations were autonomous, they were not self-supporting and in many cases not yet self-propagating or self-governing either, in the sense that they stood on their own feet, independent of assistance from Holland.

Presbyteries were organized in the late 1920's, and a synod in 1931, but the local congregations retained full authority over their own affairs.

Out of the severe testing of the Japanese occupation and the experience of revolution came a desire to draw closer in ecumenical ties with other churches. The Central Java Church met in conference with the Christian Church of North Central Java in 1949 to unite the two churches in Central Java, but for a variety of reasons the union was not permanent. The Central Java Church was one of the charter members of the Indonesia Council of Churches and has played an active role in the Council. In 1953 the Central Java Church had about 25,000 members; and the most recent statistics indicate a threefold increase in the last 15 years. How is this to be explained? It is due more to the vigorously evangelistic spirit of local congregations working in a situation where extreme political and economic instability have accentuated the disintegration of traditional social and cultural values. Many people are looking for a sounder spiritual foundation to face continuing crisis. At present the Central Java churches confront the task of nurturing the thousands of new Christians who join the church each year. Thus, in addition to its mission field in Lampang among Javanese transmigrants to South Sumatra, it faces an unprecedented challenge in evangelism and service among Muslims and former Communists in Central Java.

26   **The Java Evangelical Christian Church (Geredja Masehi Indjili di Tanah Djawa),** in the region around Mount Muria on the northern coast, has a Mennonite background. In 1851 Dutch Mennonites sent P. Jansz to Djapara, where he worked for 20 years. By the end of this period 16 men and 24 women had been baptized. These meager fruits are due partly to the fact that Islam is much more seriously embraced on the northern coast than in the central and southern parts of Java.

The missionaries attempted to establish several Christian villages (Margoredjo in 1881, Margokerto in 1901 and Pakis in 1925), but this approach was not very fruitful. The hospitals, clinics and leprosy work, however, did have considerable influence on the people. From

1928 on, more attention was paid to the towns such as Kudus and Pati where Christian nurses, teachers, civil servants and youth were gathered into congregations. Local congregations were generally led by school teachers, who were authorized to administer the sacraments. Church organization on both the local and regional level did not advance too rapidly, because Mennonite polity did not place much stress on organization. Nevertheless, in 1940 "The Conference of Javanese Congregations in Pati, Kudus and Djapara Residencies" was established. There were then 12 congregations with about 2,000 members—all adults, for the Mennonites do not practice infant baptism.

During the war this church suffered heavily both from the attacks of Muslims in the region and also at the hands of the Japanese. During the struggle for independence, however, the Muria Church proved its loyalty to the Indonesian cause and was recognized by the people in the region. In recent years American as well as European Mennonite organizations have cooperated in a variety of social, health and educational ministries as well as in evangelistic programs. The church has grown 385 percent in the last 15 years, and has 27,000 members in 16 congregations. It is a member of the Council of Churches and cooperates fully in the ecumenical movement both within and outside Indonesia. The problem of producing more and better leaders for the church is particularly urgent because of the current vigorous challenge from Islam.

27 **The Pasundan Christian Church (Geredja Kristen Pasundan)** is a small church—about 15,500 members in a West Java population of 24 million. Because Islam has put down such deep roots in Sundanese society, despite the relatively more advanced economic development of West Java, the evangelistic opportunity has been more limited than in Central and East Java.

The first missionaries from the Netherlands Missionary Association were assigned to work in the towns and cities, beginning in 1863, but the visible results were not encouraging. The congregation in Tjiandjur, after 40 years of missionary labors, consisted of slightly more than 70 persons. In Sukabumi, 10 years produced 25 members, while Bandung between 1870 and 1877 registered 25. In 1883, in Bogor, after 14 years of work, there were six Christians: four Sundanese and two Chinese.

Another method employed was for the mission to purchase a tract of land on which was established a "Christian village," where Christians who had been ostracized by their fellow villagers for embracing the Christian faith could be given land on which to settle. Thus Tjideres was created in 1877. Three other Christian villages followed by 1920, but they turned out to be ineffective in facilitating church growth.

A third approach was that of establishing schools, hospitals and orphanages. Bandung, the provincial capital, was the center of these developments, which brought many Sundanese into contact with the church and the Christian faith. Particularly effective was a students' hostel operated by a missionary couple to serve Sundanese youth studying in Bandung. Several of the present leaders of the Sundanese Church were won to Christianity through the sensitive, quiet ministry of this hostel.

Not only Sundanese but also Chinese were being reached by these missionary efforts. In 1936 nearly a third of the 6,215 members of the Sundanese Church were Chinese; but these mixed congregations had already begun to separate into Chinese and Sundanese units.

After 1885 the Pasundan Church began to be swelled by members coming from congregations established much earlier through the efforts of Mr. Anthing, a Dutch jurist in Djakarta. Believing that the Javanese could best be reached by Javanese evangelists, Anthing gave much time to discovering and training men like Sadrach. At least 50 Javanese evangelists were sent out to preach the gospel and establish congregations. The Djakarta Society for Evangelism Within and Without the Church, with which Anthing was intimately associated, gave considerable support to this effort. One result was the establishing of nearly a dozen congregations on the north coast of West Java. After Anthing died in 1883, the Netherlands Missionary Association attempted to provide pastoral care for these groups, but his successor resisted this, as Sadrach had done in Central Java. Nevertheless, within a few years members of these congregations began to find their way into the Sundanese Church.

A synod was established in 1934. As yet there were no presbyteries, but 20 congregations had been fully organized and 15 more were in process of formation. The Sundanese Church did not operate its own theological school for training ministers, but it did have training courses for evangelists. The first Sundanese minister had been ordained in 1918.

After World War II, and particularly in recent years, the church has grown at a somewhat more rapid rate as sociocultural change has accelerated in West Java. Especially following the September 30th Affair (1965), a considerable increase in evangelistic activity has occurred, sparked mainly by youth and students from various churches working in the region, and has met a promising response.

Besides the Pasundan Christian Church, many other Christian groups work in West Java. These include six member churches of the Council, the Roman Catholic Church, the Salvation Army, the Southern Baptists, the Christian and Missionary Alliance, the Seventh Day Adventists and Pentecostal groups. In the recent past a regional council of churches has been formed to coordinate cooperative efforts and to work for unity both in witness and in service to the Sundanese people. In this council the Pasundan Christian Church plays a key role.

Thus, though the field is difficult, the church of Jesus Christ, in all its diversity, is firmly rooted in West Java and is vigorously at work, particularly in the cities and towns, bringing "the gospel to all nations."

8 The Chinese and
Pentecostal Churches

Eᴵɢʜᴛ ᴏғ ᴛʜᴇ ᴍᴇᴍʙᴇʀ ᴄʜᴜʀᴄʜᴇs ᴏғ the Coun-
cil of Churches have their roots largely in the Chinese communities in
the towns and cities of Java. Some special knowledge of the background is necessary to understand the situation of these churches.[1]

The Chinese Community

Exact statistics are not available, but it is generally agreed that there
are approximately three million Chinese in Indonesia. They fall into
three groups: naturalized Chinese with Indonesian citizenship, Chinese
citizens holding Peking passports, and stateless persons of Chinese
descent who have no citizenship. Careful estimates based on available
data show one and one-half million Indonesian citizens of Chinese
ancestry and one and one-half million Chinese who are aliens. Of the
latter, at least 250,000 hold Peking passports, while more than one
million are stateless. This Chinese minority of three million constitutes
2.68 percent of the total population (112 million in 1967). The term
"Chinese" used in this context refers to those of Chinese ancestry
"who function as a member of, and identify with, Chinese society," [2] as
symbolized by the use of a Chinese surname.

96

A classification other than that based on citizenship distinguishes between China-born Chinese (called *Totok*) and Indonesia-born Chinese (called *Peranakan*). The latter form 70 percent of the Chinese community, and from them come nearly all the Indonesian citizens and most of the stateless persons. Those holding Peking passports come almost completely from the *Totok* grouping. The *Totoks* are little assimilated, primarily Chinese speaking, heavily concentrated in trade and commerce, and maintain ties with their families on mainland China. The *Peranakans,* on the other hand, are almost exclusively Indonesian speaking (reflecting greater assimilation), have few if any ties with China, and occupy white collar, managerial and professional positions as well as jobs in commerce and finance. Some *Peranakan* families have been in Indonesia for many generations. They started to come from South China before Dutch rule began at the beginning of the seventeenth century, originating primarily from Fukien and Kwangtung provinces. Large-scale immigration took place between 1860 and 1930, and the Chinese proportion of the population doubled from 1860 to 1960.

From time to time, especially during the last year or so, reports speak of discrimination and harassment against the Chinese community in Indonesia. What are the causes?

Underlying both government policies and the spontaneous anti-Chinese sentiments and actions on the part of the populace is the desire to end Chinese dominance in Indonesia's domestic economy, to overcome the self-assumed social and cultural superiority of the Chinese minority and, especially since 1965, to protect national sovereignty and honor from subversion by Chinese citizens loyal to an increasingly unfriendly Peking.

Given the historical background, present economic realities, continuing political instability, the deep resentment against the Chinese on the part of ethnic Indonesians and the growing unpopularity of the People's Republic of China among Indonesians, it is not likely that the difficulties experienced by the Chinese community in Indonesia will disappear in the near future. The long-run picture is not so bleak, however.

Skinner concludes that while the present position of Indonesian citizens of Chinese ancestry is nearly as precarious as that of alien Chinese, at least they know what is involved in their commitment to Indonesia and the task that lies before them. It is becoming increasingly common for *Peranakan* parents to give Indonesian names to their children. Indeed in the last year, under unofficial pressure from

the authorities, increasing numbers are changing their Chinese sur-
names to Indonesian names. The government has closed all schools
using the Chinese language, which means that except for the home
atmosphere, children will be in a largely Indonesian environment
henceforth. These and other developments are hastening the Indo-
nesianization of *Peranakan* culture and the steady integration of the
Peranakan social system within the larger society.

The Role of the Church

What is the relation of the Indonesian churches to this problem,
and what role can they play in the present situation?

One answer is seen in the September 11, 1966 Message of the Central
Committee of the Indonesia Council of Churches, in Section V, "The
Problem of the Chinese."

> 1. What is most urgently needed is the achievement of a sufficiently
> clear distinction between those who are alien Chinese and Indonesian
> citizens of Chinese ancestry, among other ways, by instituting Govern-
> ment regulations which make this distinction easier.
>
> 2. Towards persons who are alien Chinese living in Indonesia, the
> Government should exercise a policy based on humanitarian considera-
> tions, on our national interest, and on international conventions, and
> which will be aimed at the immediate cessation of their economic dom-
> ination over us. . . .
>
> 3. Within the process of Nation-building going on at present, the
> Government and the entire Indonesian people, including citizens of
> Chinese ancestry, should, without distinguishing ethnic group or an-
> cestry, work together responsibly towards the common future of the
> whole Indonesian Nation, if necessary leaving behind and forgetting
> past affairs.

This statement, issued by a body representing 38 Protestant
churches, speaks for a Christian constituency of more than four million Indonesians. Of these churches, seven are composed of 100,000
members who are almost wholly Indonesians of Chinese descent. In
addition it is estimated that there are at least 50,000 Chinese members
in Christian bodies not related to the Council of Churches, and 113,000
Roman Catholics from the Chinese community. This means that the
problem discussed above is of keen and daily concern to the Christian
community in Indonesia.

Of the total Chinese community in Indonesia, at least 263,000, or 8.8 percent, are Christians. Still more significant is the fact that they constitute 17.5 percent of the *Peranakan* Chinese. Thus presumably the church would be in a position to exert considerable positive influence in facilitating the process of assimilation of their membership into the larger Indonesian community. This is, in fact, going on to a significant degree.

With the exception of a small number of Chinese language congregations, almost all Roman Catholics of Chinese ancestry join with ethnic Indonesians in the life of the Catholic congregations and organizations.

On the Protestant side, seven member churches of the Council of Churches are almost wholly Chinese. The same thing is true of some Protestant bodies outside the Council. There are also, however, a number of churches and bodies, such as Methodist, Southern Baptist, Salvation Army, Bethel Full Gospel, Christian and Missionary Alliance and Pentecostal, where Chinese members join with ethnic Indonesians in local congregations and Christian organizations.

The 1954 Report of the Ministry of Religion listed 30 registered Chinese church bodies in Indonesia. But it is on Java that the development of Chinese churches with synod organizations has gone ahead furthest.

While Chinese have inhabited Indonesian islands since early colonial times, evangelistic efforts among them were not undertaken until the nineteenth century, when missionary societies became active in Indonesia. These same European societies were looking toward work on mainland China, and their earliest missionaries often spent considerable time among overseas Chinese in Southeast Asia before the doors were opened to China. The London Missionary Society and the British Missionary Society both worked among Chinese in Indonesia during the period of British control, 1811-1815. But the early baptisms of Chinese resulted not from the activity of the missionary societies but from the evangelistic efforts of individual Christians. For a long time Chinese joined other new believers in mixed congregations. They were uninvited guests, as it were, and not everywhere fully welcomed. Gradually Chinese Christians formed their own congregations, and by 1940 there were few mixed congregations left.

The earliest Chinese congregation formed in Indramaju, West Java, in 1858 when Ang Boen Swie was baptized in the local Protestant church and initiated a house church in his own home. In a few years, as other Chinese joined, they built their own sanctuary.

This pattern of a local congregation being gathered around the first person to become a Christian in the local Chinese community was fairly common. In this manner congregations formed in Purbolinggo, Central Java (1866) around Khou Tek San; in West Java, in Tjeribon (1867) around You Ong Pouw; in Sukabumi (1882) around Tjoa Beng Yang; and in Bandung (1888) around Thung Goan Hok. Most of these congregations were related to the evangelistic activities of Gan Kwee, a Chinese evangelist from Amoy, supported by the Djakarta Society for Evangelism Within and Outside the Church to work among the Chinese on Java.

In East Java, Oei Soei Tiong, baptized in 1898, became an evangelist who gathered congregations in Malang, Bangil, Modjosari and Modjokerto. He was ordained a minister in 1933.

Systematic missionary efforts among the Chinese were undertaken by various foreign societies after 1905, creating theological and ecclesiastical diversity in the Chinese churches on Java.

The American Methodist Church opened work among the Chinese in various regions: in Djakarta in 1905, in West Borneo in 1906 and in Surabaja in 1909. In 1928, however, the Methodists decided to concentrate their resources on Sumatra and withdrew from other regions. But many Chinese congregations in West Java and East Java still reflect Methodist influence, especially in their liturgy.

The Netherlands Missionary Association also worked among the Chinese in Djakarta and Surabaja. They extended assistance to Methodist-related congregations after 1928.

In Central Java around Mt. Muria the Mennonite missionaries planted the gospel among Chinese in Kudus in 1920. From the Kudus congregation there developed Chinese congregations in Djapara, Semarang, Pati and other towns. Significantly these congregations remained independent of the support and separate from the organization of the Mennonite mission.

The Gereformeerde Missionary Society assisted congregations both in North Central Java (Salatiga, Ambarawa) and South Central Java (Jogjakarta, Magelang and Solo). In each of these regions, the theological and ecclesiastical (polity) emphases of the foreign societies came to characterize the local and regional churches that developed.

It was quite common during this second period for evangelists from China to visit the Chinese communities in Java. The most influential of these was Dr. John Sung in 1937 and 1939, who attracted many thousands of Chinese to his meetings. Dr. Sung's efforts proved to be a strong stimulus to the growth of the Chinese churches in Indonesia.

There are several matters related to work with Chinese in Indonesia that should be mentioned here.

First, the evangelization of the Chinese in Indonesia was aimed primarily at the *"Singkeh"* (*Totok* or foreign-born Chinese) and was carried on in the Chinese language. But it was the *Laukeh* (*Peranakan,* or Indonesia-born Chinese) who responded best, and the congregations developed largely from this group. Most of the members are now Indonesian citizens, and the language used is Indonesian.

Second, in many cases, family groups constituted the seeds of the first congregations. When a person was baptized he sought to persuade his family and relatives to become Christians too, thus establishing strong Christian family units.

Third, from the beginning the Chinese congregations were urban in character because the Chinese, being merchants, were concentrated in the towns and cities. These churches developed in a more secular, sophisticated atmosphere and faced a different set of problems than the other churches, which were largely rural.

Fourth, because of the special status of the Chinese as the commercial class of Indonesia, their churches were on the whole in a much stronger financial position than other churches. This is reflected in the buildings, appointments and programs of local congregations.

And finally, efforts were exerted quite early to establish a unified Chinese church in Indonesia, but they have not yet borne the desired

Region	Origin	Members	Congregations	Ministers	Evangelists
West Java Synod	Reformed	4,900	12	10	4
Djakarta Synod	Methodist	2,000	5	5	2
Central Java Synod	Gereformeerde	2,950	14	9	7
Muria Synod	Mennonite	900	6	4	1
East Java Synod	Methodist and Reformed	2,900	17	6	6
Makassar	Reformed and C.M.A.	575	2	3	3
Kalimantan	Swiss Reformed and C.M.A.	600	3	1	2
Moluccas	Reformed	150	2	1	–
Bangka-Biliton	C.M.A.	275	3	2	1
East and South Sumatra	Methodist	1,300	12	4	3
TOTALS		16,550	76	45	29

fruit. Numerous conferences were held, beginning in 1926, to explore the possibility of establishing one Chinese church. But the most that could be accomplished was the formation in 1949, on the eve of the birth of the Indonesia Council of Churches, of a Council of Chinese Christian Churches in Indonesia *(Dewan Geredja-Geredja Kristen Tionghoa di Indonesia)*. The following figures, taken from their report to the founding assembly of the Council of Churches, reveal the extent of the Christian movement among Chinese in Indonesia in 1950.

Recent Developments

After Independence, in response to the growth of nationalist sentiments and the increasingly exposed position of the economically dominant Chinese minority, these Chinese churches took steps to become more Indonesian. Since most of the members were Indonesian citizens, the name was changed from Chinese *(Chung Hua Chi To Chiao Hui)* to Indonesian *(Geredja Kristen Indonesia)*, the Christian Church of Indonesia. These churches also sought closer relations with the other churches in Indonesia.

Since 1960, the East, Central and West Java Synods of the Indonesia Christian Church have been exploring ways to unite in a single organization. First steps have already been taken, and this development could possibly occur within the next decade.

It remains to indicate the present state of these churches based on the most recent statistics available.

28   The East Java Indonesia Christian Church (**Geredja Kristen Indonesia, Djawa Timur**) has a membership of 15,000 in nine congregations served by 10 ordained ministers.

29   The Central Java Indonesia Christian Church (**Geredja Kristen Indonesia, Djawa Tengah**) has a membership of 16,000 in 26 congregations served by 36 ordained ministers.

30   The West Java Indonesia Christian Church (**Geredja Kristen Indonesia, Djawa Barat**) has a membership of about 20,000 in 30 congregations served by 29 ordained ministers.

31   The Church of Christ (Geredja Kristus) has a membership of 4,000 in eight congregations served by five ministers.

32   The United Muria Christian Church of Indonesia (Persatuan Geredja-Geredja Kristen Indonesia di Muria) has a membership of 5,000 in 12 congregations served by six ordained ministers.

Few churches in Indonesia have the ratio of ministers to congregations shown above for the three Indonesia Christian Church synods: 64 ordained ministers for 70 congregations. This possibly reflects the stronger economic base in the Chinese churches; they are able to provide the support necessary for the theological education of their pastors and can pay their pastors adequately. But it also reflects the urban setting of the Chinese churches. They require a well-educated, full-time ministry since the members have better than average education by Indonesian standards. It may also result from the fact that the Chinese churches have been relatively more free of missionary control than most other churches in Indonesia and are therefore more truly autonomous. But whatever the reasons, the Chinese churches do stand out in this regard.

The Chinese, too, seem to be participating in the increased accessions reported by churches in Indonesia. A recent *Fides* report mentions new interest on the part of Chinese in Catholicism in various parts of Indonesia. In southwest Kalimantan, many motives seem to apply: "Mistrust of Chinese Communism, especially since the Chinese Cultural Revolution; the interest the Church has shown, especially since Vatican II, in social, racial and economic problems; the shortcomings of the Indonesian Constitution on human and religious questions; and esteem for the strong organization of the Catholic Archdiocese of Pontianak." (*Fides,* June 7, 1967). The third is probably not so much "shortcomings in the Indonesian Constitution" as in the erratic implementation of the citizenship regulations. And the fourth, "the strong organization," perhaps also reflects an increasingly close relation between the Roman Catholic Church and the Indonesian government, developed particularly during the latter years of Sukarno's rule, and is related to the special diplomatic position of the Vatican, unique among the religious groups in Indonesia. There is no doubt that, in addition to specifically religious motives underlying conversion to Christianity,

Protestant as well as Roman Catholic, wider social and cultural motivations are also operative, particularly in the case of a hard-pressed, insecure group such as the Chinese minority.

Skinner, writing from a purely sociological viewpoint, remarks that:

> The Christianization of the *Peranakans* population must be interpreted in large part as a search for security and status in a rapidly changing society. During the colonial era it meant identification with the power elite; in the period of independence it means identification with a segment of the native population which has been accepted within the national community.[3]

Under present conditions, much more threatening for the Chinese community than conditions in 1962 when Skinner wrote, there is added reason to see participation in the Christian Church as a significant means of identifying with the Indonesian people and thus hastening the process of assimilation, which provides the real long-range hope for those who have chosen Indonesia. In this respect the Christian Church in Indonesia can make an important contribution to both the majority and minority communities that are involved in the assimilation process.

Thus in the context of increased attention to religious affiliation in Indonesia, and the spotlighting of Chinese in relation to the struggle against communism in Indonesia, both resulting from the follow-up of the 1965 abortive coup, it would be safe to predict that Chinese will continue to join the church in larger numbers than before.

An important factor is the fact that the Chinese community is almost wholly urban. Therefore, the process of social and cultural change—modernization and secularization—has proceeded farther for the Chinese than for rural Indonesians. This fact suggests that of the religious options open to them, Christianity might seem the most attractive since it has had more experience in reacting to secularization and modernization than have Islam, Hinduism and Buddhism. Undoubtedly the ecumenical character of the church is a consideration for the *Peranakan* Chinese, who as a group have had closer relations with Western people and culture than has the average Indonesian.

Two final developments should be considered. First, in recent years, especially after 1965, Chinese Protestant congregations have been accepting increasing numbers of ethnic Indonesians into their membership, and Chinese have been joining ethnic Indonesian congregations. This is an indication that the process of assimilation is going forward from both directions. If ethnic Indonesians did not feel that the outlook and loyalties of Chinese Christians were essentially Indonesian, they would hardly join Chinese congregations.

The other development is the growing spirit of unity among the Protestant churches and the proposals for church union presently under negotiation on the national and regional levels. This trend is almost certain to grow steadily stronger in the years to come. It will bring Chinese Christians into much closer contact with Indonesians and will further the progress of assimilation, which requires active participation from both sides.

The Pentecostal Churches

The Chinese churches and the Pentecostal churches have been combined in one chapter simply because the Pentecostal expression of Christianity in Indonesia has grown widespread roots in the Chinese community, especially among the *Peranakan* grouping. This is true despite the fact that *Peranakan* Chinese are among the most secularized and Westernized Indonesians!

Very little has been written about the Pentecostal movement as a whole in Indonesia. A brief sketch is added here to what was said in Chapter 3 because three of the Pentecostal bodies have become members of the Council of Churches.

Pentecostal groups appeared in Indonesia in the late 1920's, quite possibly related to the International Church of the Four Square Gospel (Los Angeles) and the Assemblies of God (Springfield, Missouri). At the beginning it took root in East Java—Surabaja and Malang. The emotional atmosphere of Pentecostalism found a response particularly among the Eurasians, nominal members of the Protestant church who felt neglected and insecure. Later numbers of *Peranakan* Chinese were attracted for similar reasons. Pentecostalism has spread widely to Sumatra, Sulawesi and East Indonesia. In the 1953 Ministry of Religion listing of non-Roman religious bodies in Indonesia, of the 166 registered bodies 34 were Pentecostal. The most recent estimate of church statistics gives the nonconciliar Pentecostals 900,000 members and the three Pentecostal churches in the Council 438,000 members, but these figures are probably considerably inflated.

Several distinctive characteristics of the Pentecostals may be related to this rapid growth. First, laymen who manifest the gifts of the Holy Spirit have, from the beginning, played a central role in the spontaneous expansion of the movement. Theological education has not been stressed as a qualification for the ministry but rather evangelistic zeal, speaking in tongues and the power of spiritual healing, considered to be authentic marks of God's call. A highly emotional, revivalist atmosphere of spontaneity in worship and witness characterizes all activities. Third, speaking in tongues and the power of spiritual healing are highly prized. Fourth, there is almost a total lack of interest in social problems. Personal salvation, the second coming of Christ, spiritual nourishment and faithfulness in witness are the main emphases. Also, there has been little continuing relationship with overseas bodies, at least few overt organizational ties. There are, however, occasional evangelists and healers who come for shorter or longer visits. Some groups in other countries, particularly the United States, send gifts to help with buildings and equipment for witness.

In the past few years attempts to bring these bodies together in some form of cooperation have not been entirely unsuccessful. The largest groups seem to be the Assemblies of God *(Sidang Djumat Allah)*, outside the Council, and the Bethel Full Gospel Church, a Council member.

33   **The Church of Jesus the Messiah (Geredja Isa Almaseh),** an autonomous church from the beginning, was the first Pentecostal body to join the Council of Churches, in 1960. It has been instrumental in leading others into the ecumenical movement, and in so doing has made a significant contribution both to the Council of Churches and to the Pentecostal churches concerned. The Church of Jesus the Messiah came into being in Semarang, Central Java, on December 18, 1945 in a borrowed theater with 67 persons present. The mother congregation in Semarang erected its sanctuary in 1950 and, under the leadership of the Reverend Tan Hok Tjoan, grew rapidly until in 1967 it had 12 congregations, five branch groups and 20 Sunday schools, with a total membership of 5,000, of whom 1,600 were adults. Youth and Sunday school work have from the beginning been especially emphasized in this church, which in 1967 listed 12,000 members in 12 cities, all but one on Java. A theological academy was opened in 1967 to begin to meet the urgently felt need for better trained pastors. The Church of Jesus the Messiah has no formal ties with overseas bodies, but frequently receives visits and assistance from evangelists who hold revival meetings, a standard aspect of church life for these Pentecostal bodies.

34 The Bethel Full Gospel Church (Geredja Bethel Indjil Sepenuh) is a national church with headquarters in Djakarta. In 1964 when it joined the Council of Churches it reported a membership of 100,000 and 500 congregations on Java, Sumatra and Irian Barat. This body, which is related to the Bethel Temple Society in the United States, like the following one, is quite similar in teachings and liturgy to the Church of Jesus the Messiah. In organization, however, it seems to have a strong sense of local congregational autonomy.

35 The Surabaja Pentecostal Church (Geredja Pentekosta Surabaja) is similar in most regards to Bethel, but its congregations are limited to the East Java region. The only figures available indicate a membership of 20,000.

These Pentecostal churches seem to be growing rapidly, with members coming largely, but by no means entirely, from the Chinese community. It may be expected that more of them will enter into cooperation with the churches in the Council in the years ahead.

FOOTNOTES

1. For a fuller account of this background, see the writer's article in *China Notes*, July 1967 (Asia Department, National Council of the Churches of Christ in the U.S.A.)

2. Cf. G. W. Skinner, "The Chinese Minority," in R. McVey (ed.), *Indonesia*. New Haven: Human Relations Affairs Press, 1963, p. 97.

3. Skinner, *op. cit.*, p. 108. Without detracting from the value of a sociological interpretation, I would point out that the Christianization of the Peranakans is also a result of the failure of the traditional Chinese religion to satisfy their need for meaning in life.

9 Ecumenical Dimensions

T HE TERM "ECUMENICAL" IS USED in this chapter to designate those churches and bodies that participate in and cooperate through the Indonesia Council of Churches. Except where specified otherwise, it does not include either the Roman Catholics or those belonging to bodies outside the Council, though ideally all these bodies should be encompassed by the term. The reality is still far from the ideal; practice lags far behind theory. Nevertheless, the ecumenical panorama is impressive.

Background

The ecumenical movement in Protestant Christianity resulted from the success of missionary efforts to establish churches in mission lands. But ecumenical cooperation within Indonesia and with overseas churches could develop only when Indonesian churches became autonomous, not just in name but in reality. The road leading to autonomy is an important and interesting one.

Indonesian churches were planted and nourished, financed and administered by foreign missionary societies or other bodies, such as the Netherlands East India Company and the Dutch colonial government, until the Japanese occupied the Indies in 1941. From 1906 there had been a Missions Consulate in Djakarta to represent the various mission societies in their relations with the colonial government in regard to comity agreements and other matters. A number of the churches were granted autonomy during the 1930's, but because of continuing financial dependence and colonial rule, there was insufficient development of selfhood to alter the picture substantially.

World War II rudely shattered the customary order. The German attack on Holland in 1940 resulted in the internment of all German missionaries in Indonesia. The Japanese occupation of the archipelago in 1941 removed all Dutch and American personnel and financial aid. The churches were on their own; and as we have seen, they grew in spite of extreme adversity.

This severe testing, together with the revolutionary struggle for Independence (1945-1949), moved the churches forward a giant step toward achieving full selfhood. Further steps had to be taken when, in 1950, the government abolished financial subsidies to the churches and the churches were forced into independence. The fact that within a very short time the Indonesian churches became fully self-governing, self-propagating and largely self-supporting reflects the quality of missionary assistance they had received in earlier years.

The final steps to full maturity have been undertaken in the years since 1950, and they continue as the Indonesian churches draw together in various forms of ecumenical cooperation. These steps have led the churches to search for and experiment with new forms of mission through ecumenical relations. Both the "older churches" in the West and the "younger churches" in Indonesia have to grow and change in order to achieve a relationship of equals, both in status and responsibility. This is now taking place, but not without "growing pains" for all parties. It is happening in a period of radical change in the traditional relationships of church to society, of Western nations to Indonesia, of Western culture to Indonesian culture. Undoubtedly this revolutionary environment has provided one of the stimuli for the rapid growth of the ecumenical movement in Indonesia.

Ecumenical Cooperation

The dimensions and structures of ecumenical cooperation in Indonesia have recently been described in another book.[1] Only a brief summary can be given here of the ecumenical landscape.

The Indonesia Council of Churches (*Dewan Geredja-Geredja di Indonesia*), established by 27 Protestant churches in 1950, is the most representative of the ecumenical agencies. During its 18 years it has grown in size and in the functions it is called upon to perform. Foremost of these is the aim, fixed at its inauguration, to lead the Protestant churches and bodies in Indonesia in becoming a unified church. Envisaged as a center for conversation, planning and joint action on common concerns for the member churches, the Council through its five Departments and eighteen Commissions seeks to assist member churches in particular program areas, especially in witness and service, in gathering and distributing the fruits of study and research, and in developing resources, particularly personnel and facilities. The Council also serves as liaison instrument, where needed, with Indonesian government and society and with churches and Christian bodies overseas.

Other ecumenical agencies serve functional needs of the churches in particular fields. Probably the most broadly based of these is the Indonesia Bible Society (*Lembaga Alkitab Indonesia*), which serves the entire Protestant community in Indonesia, not just that part encompassed by the Council of Churches. The Bible Society's task is the translation, publication and distribution of the Scriptures in Indonesian and regional languages. In 1966, a total of 426,401 pieces were distributed.

The Christian Publishing Body (*Badan Penerbit Kristen*), like the Bible Society based in Djakarta and continuing the efforts of many years, undertakes the preparation (either original writing or translation), publication and distribution of literature required by the Christian community to grow and serve as it should. In 1965 the Christian Publishing Body, which works closely with the Committee on World Literacy and Christian Literature (LIT-LIT) of the National Council of Churches in the U.S.A., published 137 titles. These totaled more than three million pieces for a Christian community of seven million in a total population of 112 million with an average literacy rate of 65 percent.

A Christian political party (PARKINDO) and half a dozen mass organizations serving women, youth, farmers, labor, intellectuals, artists and students seek to relate Christian faith and ethics to all areas of secular life as well as to bring Christian witness and service to bear on the national life. It is through these channels that many Christians seek to participate actively, constructively and critically in the political, social, economic and cultural dimensions of nation building.

In the field of press and periodicals the Christian community has since 1961 been represented by a daily newspaper, *Sinar Harapan* ("Ray of Hope"), with a circulation of 90,000, and since 1963 by a popular monthly magazine, *Ragi Buana* ("Leaven of the World"), which reaches thousands all over the country.

The problems and opportunities related to these newer forms of witness and service are reflected in the following sentences from the Message of the Central Committee of the Indonesia Council of Churches in October, 1966.

> After analyzing the present problems concerning the Church, political parties and mass organizations, we emphasize the following. . . . 1) The Church is not a political party or a mass organization and may not be identified with a political party or mass organization. 2) . . . members are called to be faithful and obedient witnesses of Christ in the midst of society, nation and state, both as individuals and as organizations. 3) The Church is called to serve, to give guidance, instruction, counsel and where needed, warning to its members who are members both of the Christian Political Party or Mass Organizations. . . .

Finally there are specialized institutions to meet particular needs in church and society. Not all Christian universities and theological seminaries in Indonesia are ecumenical in conception and sponsorship, but the best ones are.

In the field of Christian higher education three of the several Protestant universities are well established and have received government certification. Nommensen University, serving the churches of North Sumatra, was founded in 1954 with cooperation from the Lutheran World Federation. The Christian University of Indonesia in Djakarta, founded the same year after the pattern of the *Vrije Universitet* in Amsterdam, now has six faculties and nearly 2,000 students. *Satya Watjana* Christian University in Central Java, sponsored and controlled by 18 churches in the Council of Churches, enjoys ecumenical cooperation with Dutch, German, Australian and American Churches (through the United Board for Christian Higher Education in Asia). In 1966, when it was granted full certification by the Ministry of Education, it enrolled 1,000 students from all over Indonesia in its five faculties and 11 departments. To date only Nommensen and Satya Watjana have their own campuses.

In the field of theological education there are 12 institutions for the training of clergy and Christian educators, enrolling 774 students in 1966. Of these, five are "higher schools" providing instruction at the university level, four are academies and four are Bible schools training evangelists. Only four are broadly ecumenical. The Higher Theological School in Djakarta, established in 1935, serves all the Indonesian churches. Its enrollment in 1967 was 161. The Theological School of East Indonesia, founded in 1948 and moved to Makassar in 1953, enrolled in 1967 118 students from 16 churches in eastern Indonesia. The Theological Faculty of Nommensen University, founded in 1954, serves students from five churches in North Sumatra. *Duta Watjana* Higher Theological School in Jogjakarta is a new joint effort which in 1963 combined schools in East Java and Central Java that served eight churches, which in 1966 sent 55 students.

Since American churches undertook ecumenical cooperation in Indonesia on an increased scale beginning in 1950, primary emphasis has been given to programs to educate pastors and teachers. And leadership training will continue to be given top priority in the years immediately ahead.

The Life and Mission of the Churches

In 1966, following the abortive coup on October 1, 1965, with its bloody aftermath involving hundreds of thousands, including many Communists and their suspected sympathizers, Indonesia entered a new phase of its revolution. Its leaders speak of "a new order" replacing "the old order," which brought political conflict, economic disintegration and spiritual frustration to the people. In the new order top priority is given to establishing political stability and achieving economic rehabilitation.

The churches in Indonesia have responded to the opportunities and needs manifest in this new situation in three dimensions: witness, service and unity.

The dimension of witness has been expressed in two directions simultaneously. First, Indonesian church leaders are keenly aware of the need for Christian witness in the social, political, economic and cultural spheres. How is God's word relevant in nation building—in the crisis of power, the horror of massacre, the struggle against injustice and oppression? A September, 1966 message from the Central Committee of the Council of Churches to Indonesian churches and society dealt forthrightly with such issues:

> The Church has been placed by God in the midst of the peoples, nations and societies to carry out its prophetic calling, which means the

obligation to express what is in keeping with, and what is contrary to the will of God in the life of a people and state.

The participation of Christians in efforts to restore the life of our state and society must first of all be positive and creative. We must plant a true sense of responsibility and of discipline in our people's breast. . . .

The participation of Christians must also be critical and realistic because we know that injustice and oppression basically are rooted in the heart of man himself. Therefore an opportunity for criticism and correction that is responsible and constructive must be a non-negotiable part of the life of the people. . . .

In light of our experiences with the use and misuse of power, we must be keenly aware that power is needed in every society to order its life . . . to establish justice, to punish evil and to serve the welfare of the people. Since this power is always held in the hands of sinful men, in employing it man is always threatened by the danger of misusing it for personal interests of those of one's own group. It is only possible to employ power responsibly if there is humility. Every holder of power is continually threatened by the danger of losing his humility and becoming arrogant. Consequently, we need to remember that the opportunity to use power is a gift of God who demands faithfulness and continuous self-criticism.

Second, in the area of proclamation of the gospel to individuals, accounts have been coming in that reveal an almost unprecedented situation. Thousands of people in various regions are presenting themselves for instruction in the faith and baptism into the Christian community. Some come out of disillusionment with their traditional faiths (animism, Hinduism or Islam) ; some out of fear of being branded atheist (Communist) ; some out of awareness that in a time of revolutionary change some firm direction and lasting values are essential; some out of recognition that for man on his own (secularist or Communist) there is no salvation, no hope, no joy, no strength to go on in suffering and frustration; some because of what they have seen in Christians.

From the village of Tiglingga in North Sumatra, for example, reports say that 15 ministers from six different communions joined in baptizing more than 2,000 people into one church on a Sunday in June, 1966. Several local congregations in Central Java have doubled their membership during 1966. The General Secretary of the Council of Churches, the Rev. S. Marantika, after giving instruction to a group of former Communist leaders in a Djakarta prison, baptized more than 20 in October, 1966. In some areas the number of people registering for instruction and baptism is so large that local congregations have been mobilized to the limit to provide the needed ministry.

The primary emphasis, it appears, may need to be shifted for a time from evangelism to nurture, in order to meet this new situation responsibly.

In addition to existing ministries, a number of "untouched" or "neglected" fields, both geographical, such as the island of Sumbawa, and functional, such as urban and industrial ministries, are pressing for attention.

The tide of Christian witness, both personal and social, is flowing strongly and authentically in Indonesia today. Every indication points to an increase of witness, which surely must lead to renewal. The theme of the Sixth Assembly of the Council of Churches, which opened on October 29, 1967, in Makassar, was "Behold, I make all things new" (Rev. 21:5), with "The renewal of man, church and society" as the subtheme.

In its 1966 Christmas Message, the Council said:

> Therefore, let us press forward firmly in our efforts to renew both our private life and the structures and values in the political, social, economic and cultural fields. Thus we can be saved from irresponsible, insensitive and hypocritical living, as well as from new forms of injustice in society. In the midst of the wrestlings of our people concerning the reality of the new humanity, new society, new world, the Church must be aware that it can only make a contribution if the repentance begins within the Church itself. The Church must renew its own life, its own faith, its own faithfulness to the Lord of the Church, Jesus Christ, whose advent amongst men we celebrate today.

The dimension of service is the second part of the response of Indonesian Christians to the new opportunities and needs. For more than 10 years the Council of Churches' Interchurch Aid Commission, in cooperation with various national Church World Service agencies, has been helping people visited by catastrophe—drought, famine, flood, earthquakes, volcanic eruptions and epidemics. Within the last few years the program has begun to include some pilot projects to stimulate local initiative in economic development. There is increasing need and opportunity for this kind of approach to physical rehabilitation through projects to increase agricultural production, to develop home and village industries, to provide assistance for family planning programs, public health and the like. Aid from outside can accomplish significant, though limited, objectives. Indeed foreign aid may harm more than help, if not administered in such a way as to develop local initiative, self-respect, creativity and new skills. The Interchurch Aid

Commission, in cooperation with Church World Service, among others, will place more emphasis on economic development in its expanded program for the coming years.

The dimension of unity. Ever since its creation, the Council of Churches has wrestled with the task of furthering unity among the churches in Indonesia. There have been some encouraging advances among the Chinese churches and the Javanese churches, as well as in the Protestant Church of Indonesia, but as yet there has been no significant breakthrough. On the contrary, in at least one region, North Sumatra, a large schism occurred in 1963 in the largest communion in Indonesia.

Barriers to church unity, in Indonesia as elsewhere, are as much sociological and cultural as they are theological and ecclesiastical. Therefore, they are not significantly reduced by study papers in the Commission on Unity or by lectures on the floor of General Assembly. What can reduce them is increasing common efforts by the churches in witness and service. Evidence over the past two years (1966-1967) suggests that this is beginning to happen in certain places.

One concrete example is the growth of regional councils of churches. For some years there has been talk of organizing regional councils, but only since the fifth Assembly of the Council of Churches in 1964 have these intentions begun to materialize. Within the last two years regional councils have begun to function in North Sumatra, West Java, Central Java, South and North Sulawesi, Kalimantan and the Moluccas. No financial aid has been available from the Council in Djakarta, so they are completely dependent on limited regional resources. This fact may guarantee that structure and program will grow out of needs felt in the regions. This development could have major positive influences on the Indonesia Council of Churches and on the movement toward unity.

Another could have even more pronounced effects. The Consultation on Unity, held in March, 1967, formulated a proposal on unity for submission to the Sixth General Assembly of the Indonesia Council of Churches in November, 1967. It provided for replacing the Council with an ecumenical synod of all the churches, whose actions on all matters of general concern would be binding on the regional churches. The proposal has been approved in principle by the Assembly, but it was felt that another triennium would be required to complete all preparatory steps.

In conclusion, two aspects of the life of the churches—finance and leadership—relate particularly to their missionary response to the new situation. The numerical strength of the Indonesian churches does not reveal much about their strength in leadership and finance.

Under colonial rule the financial needs of the Protestant church were largely provided for by the colonial government, while churches under missionary societies also received financial subsidies from overseas. Consequently there was little stimulus for growth in stewardship. Contributions and offerings were made, but they were mostly symbolic or for some particular purpose such as building or repairing a church edifice. The program or work of the congregation was not felt to be the responsibility of the members. After independence, however, outside subsidies were cut off (as with the Protestant church) or sharply reduced (as with churches related to foreign missionary societies), forcing the growth of a sense of stewardship sufficient to meet the minimal needs of the local budget. But there is very little for the larger life and work of the church. Most ecumenical enterprises (the Council of Churches, theological seminaries, Christian universities, the Christian Publishing Body and the Indonesian Bible Society) still rely heavily on support from abroad. This fact is a source of present, as well as potential, problems. The challenge to mission demands greater attention to this aspect of the life of the church.

So too, under colonial rule, the leadership of the churches was the responsibility of foreign missionaries. Indonesian workers were trained before 1940, but seldom to be more than assistants. Since Independence heartening growth, both quantitative and qualitative, has occurred in theological education. The situation in Christian higher education is even more remarkable. Nevertheless, at present almost every church in Indonesia faces a crisis in leadership. First, there are not enough ministers, catechists and evangelists to serve existing congregations, especially in light of exploding new growth. Hundreds of teachers of Christian religion are needed for public and parochial schools, which are required by law to provide religious instruction to students from first grade through university. The Armed Forces have requested 300 more Protestant chaplains to serve the military establishment, one of the most promising missionary opportunities today. In many churches, older ministers are reaching retirement age faster than young ministers can be educated to take their places. Moreover, in some churches leadership is still in the hands of older men trained during colonial times, who recognize the need for change but cannot transcend the traditional pattern of leadership, which is no longer adequate in the rapidly changing scene. Consequently serious tensions frequently develop between older and younger ministers.

These matters are not called to attention to give the impression that Indonesia churches are without leadership. Christ has raised up some striking figures in his service in Indonesia. But the present level of challenge and opportunity calls for many more.

The Conciliar Churches' Relations with Other Christian Bodies

In the past the Protestant churches in the Council have had almost no relations with Roman Catholic Christianity in Indonesia. Attitudes of each toward the other were negative, suspicious, fearful. Since Independence, however, and especially under the pressure of guided democracy when Christianity was in direct confrontation with both Islam and communism, Protestant and Roman Catholic groups have begun to seek cooperation, particularly in the political and social fields. Since Vatican II and the attempted coup of 1965, ecumenical relations between Protestants and Catholics have improved in a few regions, for example, the joint celebration of Christian festivals. The next years should witness further advance on this sector of the ecumenical front.

To a lesser degree the same thing has been happening in relations between conciliar churches and Protestant bodies outside the Council. Some advance may be possible in this sphere also, though in various ways the problem is a more complex one than relations with Roman Catholics.

Ecumenical Cooperation Within Indonesia

The mission societies of Western Europe, the Netherlands, Germany and Switzerland in particular, have historically been the bodies with primary responsibility for work in Indonesia. Various societies maintained work in particular regions, according to comity agreements strictly enforced by the colonial government between 1905 and 1927. But there was little formal cooperation in Indonesia or in Europe until World War II. Mention has been made of the Missions Consulate in Djakarta which, though primarily an instrument to handle relations with the colonial government, also dealt with overseas ecumenical bodies. Each European society related directly to the consul, who enjoyed diplomatic status. The Missionary Fellowship of the Netherlands Indies exerted considerable influence on developing cooperation.

The Japanese occupation (especially because it threw missionaries together in concentration camps), the revolution and Independence had as profound influences on the growth of ecumenical cooperation outside Indonesia as within. In fact it was partly the rapid development of the ecumenical movement in Indonesia, most notably the growth of the Council of Churches, that hastened and broadened ecumenical cooperation among those overseas churches.

In the early 1950's the ecumenical picture was enlarged when American churches responded to invitations to enter into cooperative projects with Indonesian churches. They had participated financially in 1940 through the Orphaned Missions program.

During the 1950's and early 1960's, ecumenical cooperation was channeled through a European and an American assigned to work as secretaries of the Commission on Mission of the Council. These secretaries, Dr. Winburn T. Thomas for the United States and a succession of Dutchmen for Europe, handled most of the administration of ecumenical cooperation between the churches and mission societies in their respective regions and the churches and agencies in Indonesia. This pattern of relationship and work meant that for a time the Commission on Mission of the Council had a larger staff and budget than did the Council itself. This consideration, along with others, necessitated a search for a better pattern of administering ecumenical relations with the Council and churches in Indonesia.

At the end of the first decade of its life, the Council of Churches had grown considerably but still could not find a full-time Indonesian secretary for its Commission on Mission. The two fraternal workers serving it were made associates to the General Secretary of the Council rather than solely to the Commission on Mission.

Meanwhile developments in Europe and America were calling for new forms of ecumenical cooperation. By 1962, when political conditions in Indonesia made closer coordination between the bodies working in Indonesia also essential, the Continental Commission for Church and Mission in Indonesia (Kontinentale Kommission für Kirche und Mission in Indonesien) was formed. When the statutes were approved early in 1965, there were seven members: The Evangelical Missionary Society in Basel, Switzerland; the Board of Foreign Missions of the Netherlands Reformed Church in Oegstgeest, Netherlands; the Mission Board of the Reformed Churches of the Netherlands in Baarn, Netherlands; the European Mennonite Evangelization Committee in Amsterdam; the Netherlands Bible Society in Amsterdam; the Reformed Missions League in the Netherlands Reformed Church in Utrecht, Netherlands; and the Rhenish Missionary Society in Wuppertal-Barmen, Germany.

> The purpose and concern of the KKKMI is the coordination and promotion of missionary-ecumenical tasks of the societies, churches, and institutions (which are members and consultants) in their fields of activity in Indonesia. The KKKMI is working in close contact and mutual consultation with the continental European Missions Councils as well as with the regional Indonesian churches and the DGI (Council of Churches). (From the Statutes of the KKKMI)

The Commission's representative in Indonesia is presently the Rev. J. Bos, who serves under the associate general secretary of the Council.

In 1963, at the suggestion of the Indonesia Council of Churches, the Continental Commission sent a five-man delegation to conduct a survey of the needs and opportunities in Indonesia and to consult with the regional churches and the Council about further ecumenical cooperation.

The development on the American side is somewhat similar, though the background is different. Before 1950 the only American church working with Indonesian bodies now in the Council of Churches was The Methodist Church. Shortly after the end of the Pacific war and before the achievement of sovereignty from the Dutch in 1949, at the initiative of both the Indonesian churches and the Dutch Missionary Council through the International Missionary Council, Presbyterian and Reformed churches in the United States were asked to consider cooperating in ecumenical mission in Indonesia. The Southeast Asia Committee of the Division of Foreign Missions (now the Division of Overseas Ministries) of the National Council of the Churches of Christ in the U.S.A. dispatched a survey team to study the needs and opportunities in Indonesia and to discover how American churches could best cooperate. The report, dated October, 1950, recommended a new cooperative program in Indonesia shared by American churches and administered by the Southeast Asia Committee through the Council of Churches in Indonesia. American churches were encouraged to work ecumenically not only in the United States but also in Indonesia, through joint programs serving all the churches in higher education, theological education, Christian literature, youth and student work.

The United Presbyterian Church in the U.S.A. was the first to assign personnel—Dr. Winburn T. Thomas, who was appointed the field representative of the Southeast Asia Committee. Other Presbyterians soon followed, as did fraternal workers from other churches. This program developed to such a degree by the early 1960's that a better organization was required. First, in mid-1963 an Indonesia Subcommittee of the Southeast Asia Committee was set up, and then by the end of 1964 an Indonesia Committee. After the reorganization of the NCCCUSA in that same year, the Indonesia Committee of the Asia Department of the Division of Overseas Ministries of the NCCCUSA was established and the Standing Rules adopted in January, 1965.

A preamble noted that the involvement of North American mission boards in Indonesia is different from that in other countries, because they entered Indonesia only after 1950 "not to establish denominational churches but to work in partnership with existing churches and Christian institutions in relationship to the total life of the Protestant churches in Indonesia." The purpose was then set forth: "The Indonesia Committee shall be the agent through which the boards engage in witness and service in partnership with churches and Christian institutions in Indonesia."

At present, representatives of 13 American churches and agencies constitute the membership of the Indonesia Committee: the American Baptist Convention, the American Bible Society, the Christian Churches—Disciples of Christ, the Church of the Brethren, the Evangelical Covenant Church, the Evangelical United Brethren Church, the Mennonite Central Committee, The Methodist Church, the Presbyterian Church in the United States, the United Board for Christian Higher Education in Asia, the United Church of Christ, the United Presbyterian Church in the United States of America, and the Young Men's Christian Association International Committee.

These bodies now have approximately 50 fraternal workers assigned to Indonesia (American societies not working with member churches in the Council have at least 250 missionaries in Indonesia).

Several units of the Division of Overseas Ministries of the NCCCUSA—the Committee on World Literacy and Christian Literature (LIT-LIT), the Radio, Visual Education and Mass Communication Committee (RAVEMCCO), the Christian Medical Council, the Committee on Agriculture and Rural Life (CARL) and Church World Service (CWS)—also work through the Indonesia Committee to assist specialized ministries in Indonesia.

In general the Indonesia Committee bears responsibility for the cooperative program in Indonesia, maintains liaison with the Council of Churches in Indonesia and its related bodies, and serves as the agency through which the member organizations determine priorities and their common policy for work in Indonesia.

As the Continental Commission in Europe and the Indonesia Committee in the United States have developed over the last few years, the need for closer coordination and cooperation has been mutually recognized. At least once a year representatives of each attend the meetings of the other, and the minutes of meetings are regularly shared. This significant development of ecumenical cooperation in Indonesia has been warmly welcomed by all parties.

Churches in Australia and New Zealand, particularly the Methodist and Presbyterian churches, have since the early 1950's cooperated with Indonesian churches in Timor and West Java as well as with various ecumenical projects of the Indonesia Council and its related bodies. This cooperation has been administered directly through the Commission on Mission and the Secretariat of the Indonesia Council.

Indonesia churches are also related to regional and world ecumenical bodies. Fourteen of the 35 Protestant churches in Indonesia are members of the World Council of Churches and participate in its assemblies and the work of its divisions. The Indonesia Council of Churches is one of the most active members of the East Asia Christian Conference, which was established in 1959 and has its headquarters in Bangkok.

Four Indonesian churches on Sumatra are closely related to the Lutheran World Federation, which since the early 1950's has contributed very large resources in funds and personnel to this region. Nine Indonesian churches are members of the World Presbyterian Alliance and through its activities come into contact with Reformed communions in all parts of the world.

In addition to contacts with Asian churches that through their councils are members of the East Asia Christian Conference, Indonesian Christian bodies have welcomed fraternal workers from India, Japan and the Philippines and have sent fraternal workers to Sarawak, Thailand and the Philippines.

Thus it can be said that Christianity in Indonesia has developed broad and deep ecumenical dimensions. These have added immeasurably to the quality of church life and ministry both in Indonesia and around the world.

Sukabumi 1967: A New Beginning?

In the West Java hill town of Sukabumi, an historic occasion occurred early in 1967. For the first time representatives of the Indonesian churches, at the invitation of the Council of Churches, met for consultations with representatives of the churches and missionary societies in North America, Europe, Australia and New Zealand that participate in ecumenical mission in Indonesia. Unity, witness, service and theological education were the subjects considered. Why call it "a new beginning"?

It was the most comprehensively attended and representative consultation that has yet taken place between churches and agencies cooperating in Indonesia. Not only was there opportunity for Indonesian church leaders to speak fully and frankly with all cooperating boards and bodies from outside Indonesia but, just as significantly, the Europeans, Americans, Australians and World Council delegates had ample opportunity to exchange views on common problems. This represents an important milestone.

A new situation has emerged in Indonesia. The church confronts new problems and vastly expanded opportunities. Interest on the part of overseas churches in cooperation with Indonesian churches has increased, both in the number willing to become involved and in the amount of involvement. The partnership in mission (witness and service) in Indonesia that has occurred over the years has more richly endowed the life and mission of the church to the world. But this new situation has made possible and requires the development of more efficient channels of cooperation in mission, within which the full selfhood and creative initiative of all partners may grow and bear maximum fruits. How shall we proceed?

One alternative, favored by some in Indonesia and overseas, would be for each overseas church or body to enter into its own cooperative relationship with the particular church body (or bodies) it chooses. This would be a sort of laissez-faire approach characterized by minimum coordination both within and outside Indonesia. This is the pattern that obtained during much of the past for most of the parties working in Indonesia. Support for this approach rests for some in their philosophy of mission, for others in their ecclesiastical character. Others may be convinced that there is no practical alternative in light of the size of the mission field in Indonesia and the weakness of the possible coordinating bodies there and abroad.

A second alternative, especially attractive to those who see the haphazardness, wastefulness and perhaps the divisiveness that would result from the first, would be to seek a maximum of comprehensive planning and coordinated administration centered in one or more locations outside Indonesia. This approach would necessarily operate through a "missions consulate" or similar base in Indonesia. A substantial measure of initiative and control would be vested in the coordinating body outside Indonesia and would be administered through its representative(s) in Indonesia. The rationale for this approach would be the requirement, arising from the Western side of the "partnership," for a rational, efficient, responsible ecumenical operation that, on the one hand, would avoid the weaknesses of the laissez-faire approach and, on the other, circumvent the planning and administrative limitations manifest in the present coordinating body in Indonesia.

A third alternative would, like the second, embody a comprehensive approach and maximum coordination between overseas agencies, but would locate the coordinating function in Indonesia and have it performed by an instrumentality of the churches there.

Given present circumstances and the development of Christian work to date, it is abundantly clear that Indonesia must be viewed and cultivated as "one mission field," as argued persuasively at the Fifth Assembly of the Council of Churches in 1964. This means, both in theory and in practice, that *all* cooperating bodies need to draw up and agree on a comprehensive plan for mission, both in witness and in service.

In view of the developing situation in Indonesia, including the level of selfhood of the churches and their ecumenical manifestations, and in view of the theory and practice of mission through ecumenical relations, it is essential that the coordination required for comprehensive planning and execution of mission in Indonesia be centered *in* Indonesia, if it is to be realistic, creative, effective and responsible. A central requirement for the planning and executing functions is that the coordinating body be able to maintain good communication both with the churches and Christian bodies in Indonesia and with the churches, agencies and ecumenical bodies overseas. Mutual understanding and trust between all parties is basic communication.

The coordinating agent will need to be created and given form *by* the churches in Indonesia. They must feel that it is theirs, and expresses their interests, their needs, their thinking and their will, especially in relation to ecumenical cooperation. They must also, however, see that it meets the needs of overseas churches in ecumenical cooperation, but that it cannot be an instrument fashioned by or primarily dependent on overseas churches. The establishment of such a coordinating agent will reflect the need and desire of the Indonesian churches for unity in witness and service. It will develop awareness that witness and service need not be in tension but are, rather, mutually supportive. Greater unity of purpose, and also of structure, will result from greater common efforts in witness and service, and vice versa.

The Indonesia Committee of the Division of Overseas Ministries of the NCCCUSA together with the Continental Commission and the Indonesia Council of Churches, seeks to move in the direction of the third alternative. This pattern of ecumenical cooperation in Indonesia would embrace the values inherent in the second alternative (a comprehensive approach effectively executed) and in the first (the mutual blessings of a bilateral relationship of some depth and continuity, but without the exclusiveness and possessiveness that have often accompanied such relationships).

Three things seem incumbent on all parties in order to develop relationships that can produce and direct the resources required to grasp present opportunities for advance in witness and service:

1. A common conception of the task and a common commitment to it;
2. Leadership competent to implement the policies and program; and
3. Procedures adequate for effective communication and financial responsibility.

All parties to this partnership in mission have as their central goal witness to Christ and service to men in his name. For this alone, all our coordinating and interlocking structures exist. Consequently, resources—human and material—should be available to such structures only so long and insofar as these function to strengthen, renew and unify the churches in Indonesia and overseas in their programs of witness and service.

FOOTNOTES
1. Gerald H. Anderson (ed.), *Christ and Crisis in Southeast Asia*. New York: Friendship Press, 1968.

Appendix A

Some Key Facts About Indonesia

Area: 738,865 square miles (44 million acres arable, 1.34 million acres irrigated).

Population: 112,000,000 (rural, 85 percent, urban 15 percent); density, 132 per square mile; rate of increase, 2.45 percent (in 1966).

Climate: Tropical.

Languages: Indonesian (official), English, Chinese, Dutch, and many regional languages.

Literacy rate: 43 percent.

Gross national product: $9,350,000,000.

Income: $85 per capita.

Government and politics: Republic. Basic Constitution of 1945; Provisional People's Consultative Council is highest policy-making body; Parliament representing eight political parties and functional groupings; acting president, General Suharto; most recent national election in 1955, next scheduled for 1968.

Religions: Muslim 85 percent; Christian 6.3 percent; Hindu-Bali 2 percent; Buddhist 0.9 percent; other 5.9 percent.

Physicians: one per 10,000 people; hospital beds, 0.8 per 10,000.

Newspapers: 95 (circulation one million).

Radio receivers: 1.2 million (13 per 1,000).

Cinema attendance: 257 million.

Appendix B

Chronology of Events in Indonesia's History

A.D. 1-900 — Indian influences, first Hindu then Buddhist, penetrate Western Indonesia and reach peak of flowering in seventh to ninth centuries in Shailendra and Srivijaya empires.

A.D. 132, 414   Early contacts with China through embassies and
and 671   pilgrims.

A.D. 1102   Earliest Muslim incription on Java.

1290   First town (Perlak in N. Sumatra) converted to
                 Islam.

1293   Chinese expedition against Kertanagara, last ruler of
                 Singhasari kingdom in E. Java, defeated finally by
                 Vijaya, first ruler of Madjapahit dynasty, which fell
                 at end of fifteenth century.

1511-1530   Portuguese arrive and establish authority in the
                 Moluccas.

1530's   Roman Catholic Christianity first introduced into
                 Indonesia in the Moluccas; 1546 Francis Xavier la-
                 bored 9 months in the Moluccas.

1605   The Dutch replace the Portuguese in the Moluccas,
                 and the Netherlands East Indies Company rule begins
                 to establish monopoly on spice trade, with great dif-
                 ficulty because of English smugglers and native
                 princes.

1799   Dutch East India Company dissolved after Holland
                 conquered by France.

1811-1816   British rule the Indies under Thomas S. Raffles.

1830-1870   van den Bosch introduces the culture system to stimu-
                 late exports of agricultural commodities, coffee, to-
                 bacco, sugar, tea, spices and other products to Holland.

1870-1910   Colonial government completes subjugation of out-
                 lying regions: Atjeh, Bali, Lombok, S. Celebes, and
                 furthers economic exploitation especially in argricul-
                 ture and extractive (oil and tin) sectors.

1908 and 1912   Establishment of first Indonesian nationalist organiza-
                 tions, *Budi Utomo* and *Sarekat Islam*.

1920   Communist party of Indonesia founded.

1926   First Communist uprising, in W. Java and W. Sumatra.

1930-1936   Economic depression causes severe hardship in Indo-
                 nesia.

1942-1945   Japanese defeat of Dutch and occupation of Indonesia.

1945   August 17, Proclamation of Independence by Sukarno and Hatta, followed by revolutionary struggle against the Dutch who sought to reimpose colonial rule by force.

1948   Second Communist insurrection, in Madiun, E. Java.

1949   December 29, Signing of Round Table Agreements in the Hague, under strong United Nations pressures, in which the Dutch recognize the sovereignty and independence of Indonesia.

1950-1959   Period of parliamentary democracy, in which the central government combats three rebellions (Republic of South Moluccas, Dar-ul Islam and PRRI-PERMESTA), holds national elections in 1955, and attempts unsuccessfully to draft a permanent Constitution.

1957   Nationalization of all Dutch enterprises in struggle over control of West New Guinea.

July, 1959-
March, 1966   Period of "guided democracy" and *NASAKOM*.

1959-1962   Struggle against the Dutch to regain control of W. Irian.

1963-1965   Confrontation against "British Malaysia."

January, 1965   Sukarno takes Indonesia out of the United Nations.

1965   The year of galloping inflation and advanced economic stagnation. October 1, Attempted coup by Revolutionary Council and assassination of 6 top Army generals, followed by massacre of hundreds of thousands of Communists and their sympathizers.

1966   March 11, Temporary transfer of authority from President Sukarno to General Suharto, later confirmed by Provisional People's Consultative Council (MPRS).

1967   February, General Suharto appointed Acting President, confirmed in March by MPRS. New government mounts vigorous attack on economic disintegration, brings Indonesia back into the United Nations and ends confrontation against Malaysia.

BIBLIOGRAPHY

Benda, H., *The Crescent and the Rising Sun*. The Hague: van Hoeve, 1958. Deals with Islam in Indonesia, especially under the Japanese occupation.

Geertz, Clifford, *The Religion of Java*. New York: The Free Press, 1959. A study of the religious life of the most populous island of Indonesia, by a noted anthropologist.

Goodfriend, Arthur, *Rice Roots*. Ithaca: Cornell University Press, 1958. The account of a sensitive American family's efforts to penetrate and understand Indonesians, their society and culture; eminently readable.

Holt, Claire, *Art in Indonesia: Continuities and Change*. Ithaca: Cornell University Press, 1967. A comprehensive survey of the fine arts from earliest times to the 1950's, by a noted expert in the field.

Kahin, George McTurnan, *Nationalism and Revolution in Indonesia*. Ithaca: Cornell University Press, 1952. The classical study of the revolutionary period (1945-50) and its background.

Koentjaraningrat, raden mas (ed.), *Villages in Indonesia*. Ithaca: Cornell University Press, 1966. The general pattern of life in sixteen different villages in various parts of Indonesia, by sociologists and anthropologists.

McVey, Ruth T. (ed.), *Indonesia*. New Haven: Human Relations Area Files (Taplinger), 1963. The best general introduction to various aspects of Indonesian society and culture; scholarly, done by specialists in their various fields.

Vlekkem, B. H. M., *Nusantara: A History of Indonesia*. The Hague: van Hoeve, 1959. A good standard work, by a Dutch scholar, on Indonesia's history.

Wertheim, W. F., *Indonesian Society in Transition*. The Hague: van Hoeve, 1959. A competent analysis of change in the various spheres of Indonesian society from the earliest colonial times to the middle 1950's; based on broad scholarship, but with a Marxist bias.